£7

The

He

This book commemorates the 350th anniversary of the Civil War conflict in Yorkshire between Sir Francis Mackworth's royalist forces and those of the parliamentarian Colonel Bradshaw in 1643

With ye compliments of Captain Helliwell

+

D. Shires

The Halifax Cavaliers and the Heptonstall Roundheads

David Shires

with Sheila King

Illustrated by Geoff Leathley

PURITAN PRESS

HALIFAX

Puritan Press

Helliwell House, Sowerby Bridge, Halifax,

West Yorkshire HX6 1PE

First published 1993

Designed by Sue Hogg

Printed and bound in Great Britain by Hart and Clough Ltd, Summerville Road, Bradford BD7 1PZ

ISBN 0 9521528 0 0

Front cover: In the background are two local landmarks. To the right is the medieval Heptonstall Church (now in ruins); to the left is the Halifax gibbet, an ancient guillotine used to execute thieves.
In the foreground an officer of Sir Francis Mackworth's royalist army engages in close combat with a parliamentary captain under the command of Colonel Bradshaw

To

Captain Helliwell,

a friend and guide for many years

Contents

Illustrations

Introduction

I wonder what William Shakespeare would have made of the English Civil War, of cavaliers and roundheads?

Sadly, the bard had long been buried when Charles, King of England, first waged war on his Parliament in 1642, so we will never know. That may be just as well, for perhaps there was more drama in England's Civil War years than even Mr Shakespeare's quill could have coped with!

I hope my pen will at least be able to re-create part of that story, the fascinating conflict in Yorkshire between the Halifax Cavaliers and the Heptonstall Roundheads.

The tale starts in July 1643, when Sir Francis Mackworth first entered Halifax with his roistering royalists, followed four months later by the arrival, at Heptonstall, of Colonel Bradshaw and his pious parliamentarians. Seven months after it began, the story ends with the departure of both armies from Halifax and Heptonstall alike, the soldiers marching off into history, taking with them the memories of hard-fought battles at Heptonstall and Sowerby Bridge, as well as skirmishes in Warley and Mixenden.

Such battles may not gain the historical heights of Edgehill or Naseby, and who knows if Sir Francis Mackworth will be remembered for as long as King Charles, or Colonel Bradshaw alongside Oliver Cromwell? Yet our seven months in 1643-44, when Halifax was a town full of royalist soldiers, rather than traffic, and Heptonstall welcomed the parliamentary army as it now does the modern-day tourist, can surely still stand as testimony that here in England, in those far-off days, there was more excitement than could ever be dreamt of in the mundane and humdrum reality of our time.

This book, which takes the form of a diary from July 1643 to January 1644, depicts local events and, where relevant, national occurrences.

It is for all who would care to capture, if just for a little while, a vision of Halifax and Heptonstall at the time of England's Civil War.

Setting the Scene

'Thou would think it strange if I should tell thee there was a time in England when brothers killed brothers, cousins cousins, and friends their friends'
Sir John Oglander, royalist

ENGLAND 1642

The time had come for brothers, cousins and friends to take up arms against each other. King and Parliament were now marching down a road which led to separate camps and civil war. Unresolved problems, ranging from religion to money, finally gave birth to the greatest question of all: who should govern England, King Charles I or his Parliament? On these issues words had been exhausted and both sides were now reaching for swords and mustering armies.

Initially the fighting took the form of 'county matches'. In Lancashire, for example, the parliamentarians, known as cropheads or roundheads, were solely concerned with defeating the Lancashire royalists, nicknamed cavaliers, who in turn confined their activities to their home county.

YORKSHIRE

The county match here was waged between the forces of the enormously wealthy Earl of Newcastle, whose commands came directly from the King, and those of the elderly Ferdinando,

Lord Fairfax, and his son, Sir Thomas, who took their orders from Parliament. Objectives were identical: to defeat the enemy and seize control of Yorkshire.

For a year towns fell first to one side then the other. Finally, upon Adwalton Moor near Bradford, on 30 June 1643, was fought the decisive battle for Yorkshire. The parliamentary forces, led by the Fairfaxes, were soundly beaten. The county match was over and the royalists victorious. In triumph the Earl of Newcastle marched into Bradford, turning a blind eye as his soldiers plundered and pillaged the town. These events took place at the beginning of July and mark the start of our story.

Sir Francis Mackworth was Major General to the Earl of Newcastle. He was ordered by the Earl to lead part of the royalist army out of Bradford and with it to occupy Halifax, which was now of great strategic importance. It was the first sizable town to be reached in a day's march from Lancashire, and definite danger threatened from that corner of the kingdom, for there the county match had been won by the parliamentarians.

Whether the King's army marched into Lancashire or his opponents attacked Yorkshire, either way, in the front line and the thick of things were destined to be the Halifax Cavaliers and the Heptonstall Roundheads.

SIR FRANCIS MACKWORTH, HIS OFFICERS AND SOLDIERS AT HALIFAX

Sir Francis Mackworth of Normanton, Rutlandshire, was at The Hague in November 1642 recruiting men. He returned to

Sir Francis Mackworth enters Halifax

England in December and in the following year was given a general command of the royalist garrisons in the West Riding, establishing his headquarters at Halifax. After the collapse of the King's cause in the north, he eventually secured leave to resume his command in the Low Countries.

Sir George Wentworth of Woolley, Yorkshire, was a lieutenant colonel commanding a regiment of cavalry. Before the war he had sat in the House of Commons as the Member for Pontefract, but had declared for the King when hostilities broke out. Because of his military activities and large wealth he was fined a sum of over £3000 by Parliament when the war ended.

Sir William Huddlestone of Millom, Cumberland, was a colonel in command of a regiment of foot. Some time during the occupation of Halifax, he left his regiment and returned home to command another force of Westmorland royalists. He was taken prisoner by Alexander Rigby's Lancashire roundheads at the Battle of Lindale on 1 October 1643.

Sir Richard Hutton of Goldsborough, Yorkshire, was a colonel commanding two regiments of foot. He had been MP for Knaresborough and was appointed Sheriff of Yorkshire in 1642. Fatally wounded at Sherburn in 1645, he died at Skipton.

Sir John Hilton of Hilton, County Durham, was a colonel in command of a regiment of foot which had been raised in Cumberland. He is known to have fought at the Battle of Marston Moor on 2 July 1644 and his loyalty to the royalist cause was to cost him a fine of £484 12s after the war.

The cavaliers at Halifax who were commanded by these officers came mostly from the four northern counties of Cumberland, Westmorland, Northumberland and the Palatinate of Durham, for at the beginning of the war the royalist gentry of Yorkshire had insufficient forces. They had sought assistance from the Earl of Newcastle, who, in turn, persuaded his soldiers, upon promise of pay, to leave their own areas (where no threat from the enemy existed) and fight the parliamentarians of Yorkshire.

COLONEL BRADSHAW, HIS OFFICERS AND SOLDIERS AT HEPTONSTALL

Colonel Robert Bradshaw of Bradshaw, near Bolton, Lancashire. In 1642 the Earl of Derby, who commanded the Lancashire royalists, lay siege to the parliamentarian stronghold of Manchester. Captain Radcliffe and the then Captain Bradshaw held joint command in defence of the town. During an assault upon Manchester, 'a cannon bullet came so near Captain Bradshaw as it touched his arm, but hurt him not.' Described as a 'very wise, valiant and religious man', he died at Heptonstall on 8 December 1643.

Major Eden was second in command of the Heptonstall Garrison, taking full command after the death of Colonel Bradshaw. He fought with Lord Fairfax's army in 1645 as it lay siege to the royalist garrison of Pontefract Castle. During the siege, on 14 April, 'a sortie was made from the castle by one William Belwether and six kindred spirits', who rushed on the trenches near Bread Lane End. A fierce fight followed and in the darkness an officer dressed in a black scarf and buff coat, presumed to be Major Eden, was killed.

Captain Farrer was a soldier even before the war, retained in military service for the purpose of training militia men in

Colonel Bradshaw enters Heptonstall

warfare. Together with Captain Beaumont, he drilled and instructed the men of Halifax and the surrounding area. At the outbreak of hostilities, because of their differing allegiances the two officers were to part company. Thomas Beaumont supported the King and became Governor of Sheffield Castle, whereas Captain Farrer took up arms for Parliament.

Captain Taylor of Brighouse, Yorkshire, was a wealthy man and a follower of George Fox, the Quaker. In 1836 workmen digging a drain discovered Captain Taylor's grave. He had been buried, standing upright by the side of his wife and daughters, in the garden of his house in Brighouse.

Captain Helliwell of Lancashire. Little if anything is known of this officer in the Heptonstall army. Readers are referred, however, to the pages at the end of this book.

The roundheads at Heptonstall who were commanded by these officers were mostly Yorkshiremen who had been exiled in Lancashire after the Battle of Adwalton Moor (30 June 1643), although at least two companies originated from Lancashire. The army was composed of fewer than 850 soldiers and civilian volunteers, 500 of whom were armed with nothing more than pitchforks or other farming implements. Even so, this was essentially an offensive force, sent from Lancashire to start a small localized campaign specifically directed against the cavaliers at Halifax.

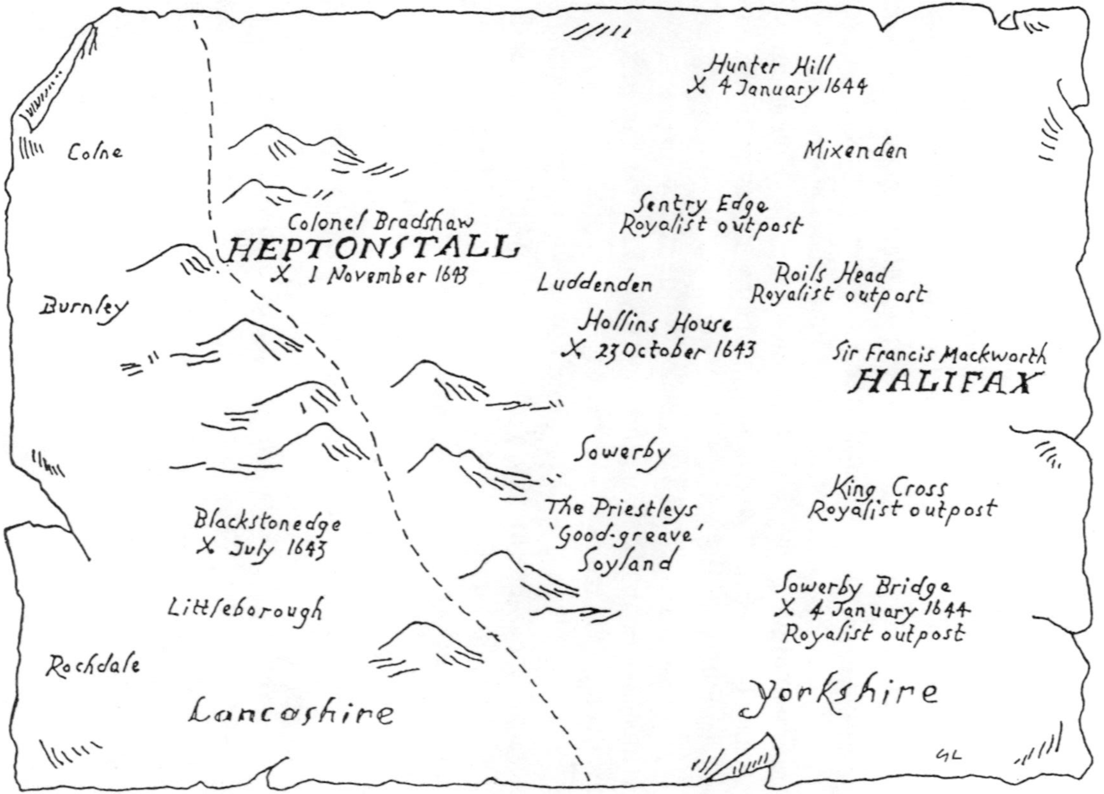
Hunter Hill
X 4 January 1644
Colne
Mixenden
Colonel Bradshaw
HEPTONSTALL
X 1 November 1643
Sentry Edge
Royalist outpost
Luddenden
Roils Head
Royalist outpost
Burnley
Hollins House
X 23 October 1643
Sir Francis Mackworth
HALIFAX
Sowerby
The Priestleys
'Good-greave'
Soyland
King Cross
Royalist outpost
Blackstonedge
X July 1643
Littleborough
Sowerby Bridge
X 4 January 1644
Royalist outpost
Rochdale
Lancashire
Yorkshire
GL

CHAPTER ONE

July 1643

Sir Francis Mackworth enters Halifax - The Halifax refugees - Yorkshire's demand for Lancashire's surrender - The advanced royalist outposts - The upkeep and maintenance of General Mackworth's army - Lancashire's refusal to surrender and the fortification of its border frontiers - The Blackstonedge skirmish - The Earl of Newcastle's army marches into Lincolnshire

After his victory at Adwalton Moor, the Earl of Newcastle laid siege to Bradford. Sir Thomas Fairfax attempted to hold the town but failed and retreated to Hull. Consequently on 3 July Bradford fell to the cavaliers. The next day Halifax was to share the same fate . . .

TUESDAY, 4TH

As the royalist general Sir Francis Mackworth rode out of Bradford towards Halifax on or about this day, despite leading a formidable force consisting of a regiment of horse and four regiments of foot, perhaps his thoughts betrayed a certain uneasiness as he reflected upon orders given to him by His Excellency the Earl of Newcastle. He had been commanded not only to occupy a town with an army the citizens would neither want nor welcome, but also to guard and defend all the western approaches leading to and from the county border. Here the Yorkshire royalists would inevitably face the Lancashire parliamentarians, and both sides, with equal and grim determination, were preparing for conflict and bloodshed.

The cavalry troopers, pikemen and musketeers who marched with Sir Francis, not having his burden of command, may well have been more carefree, for had they not, but a few days before, utterly routed the Fairfaxes upon Adwalton Moor? And with saddlebags and knapsacks full of plunder from Bradford, did they not believe Halifax would hold more of the same?

Troubled minds or not, with drums beating and banners flying the royalist army marched on, but not without opposition along the way. On the final descent into the town a few of Fairfax's determined diehards appear to have made a valiant last stand with cannon and shot. A sword, cannon balls and horseshoes found on the hillside directly to the north of Halifax bear testimony to a skirmish. Nevertheless, although the parliamentarians disputed Sir Francis Mackworth's entrance into Halifax, they were unable to halt it.

*

As puritans who sympathized with Parliament, and with the certainty of the enemy's approach sooner or later, most of the townsfolk had already gathered together what possessions they or a horse and cart could carry. Both rich and poor alike made a pitiful procession as they took to the high moorland roads winding over the hills into Lancashire. Phoebe Lister of Shibden Hall buried the deeds of her home, then departed for Manchester, escorted perhaps by the minister of Halifax

The Halifax refugees

Church, the Reverend Henry Roote. He may also have conducted Mrs Lister's funeral service, for she died in Manchester just seven months later.

John Brearcliffe, a twenty-five-year-old apothecary, went to Bury where he met his future wife Dorothy Meadowcroft. In October he was to return to Yorkshire with Colonel Bradshaw, possibly as the army surgeon. Later he wrote the first account of the Halifax Cavaliers and the Heptonstall Roundheads.

The Yorkshire refugees would shortly swell the towns of East Lancashire; towns such as Burnley, Colne, Rochdale, Bury and Heywood, where friends, relatives and well-wishers gave them safe haven, hoping all the while for better times for the parliamentary cause.

WEDNESDAY, 5TH

From Bradford the Earl of Newcastle fired the first warning shot towards the enemy in Lancashire, but only in the form of a summons of surrender to the officers and soldiers in Manchester.

> I presume you are not ignorant of the success it hath pleased Almighty God to give unto His Majesty's army under my command [referring to his victory at Adwalton Moor]. . . . His Majesty is graciously pleased to authorise me to receive you into his favour and protection, which I am willing to do, as to inforce your obedience if you refuse. . . . My condition is such that I need not court you . . . let me receive your answer by this messenger.

As the Earl's messenger galloped away to deliver Yorkshire's threat, Sir Francis Mackworth was establishing his headquarters and deploying his army.

*

It was essential to watch for the enemy's approach from Lancashire and to this end soldiers were sent out westwards towards Warley Town, to garrison Roils Head and the ridge of high ground now known as Sentry Edge, strategic vantage points overlooking Luddenden Valley and the road to Burnley and Colne.

Lieutenant Colonel Wentworth, with his regiment of cavalry, occupied King Cross and Sowerby Bridge to guard against the threat from Manchester and Rochdale.

As military preparations were being made, the people of Halifax and the surrounding townships who had not yet fled to the sister county were also preparing themselves. The King's army was very demanding for its upkeep and maintenance, and the burden would fall unfairly and squarely on them. Soldiers required billets and received 'free quarter', which meant the householders lodging them were given not money, but vouchers to be redeemed for cash at a later date, if and when the King was victorious.

Fixed sums were levied in an attempt to provide regular money for soldiers' pay, and the Petty Constables of Halifax, men such as Jo. Hodgson the Butcher, Richard Denton the Badger and James Foxcroft, innkeeper of the Swan, had the unenviable task of collecting the assessments. Those who could not or would not pay faced fines, imprisonment or seizure of goods, plate, horses and cattle.

In his memoirs, John Hodgson, a captain under Fairfax, gave an account of what people and townships could expect whenever the Earl of Newcastle and his mighty army marched forth. 'It was observed by some, that the land was like Eden before him, and behind him as a barren wilderness.'

As the royalist soldiers commanded by General Mackworth settled down to the occupation of Halifax, the inhabitants began to suffer hardship and hunger resulting from the despoiling of their own lands by a voracious and unsympathetic army.

FRIDAY, 7TH

From Manchester came the resolute answer from the commanders-in-chief to the Earl of Newcastle's demand that they lay down their arms.

> . . . Sir, we are nothing dismayed at your force, but hope that God, who hath been our Protector hitherto, will so direct our just army, that we shall be able to return the violence intended into their bosoms, that shall assay the prosecution of it, which shall be the endeavour of His Majesty's most humble and obedient subjects.

*

Manchester, the parliamentarian stronghold of Lancashire, was to answer the Earl not only in pen and ink, but with force of arms. An application was made to the Parliament in London for '40 barrels of powder and some few arms . . . to preserve our town and whole county.'

Two thousand men were sent to Rochdale, 800 of whom were garrisoned upon the bleak moors of Blackstonedge, there to defend the Lancashire border and secure the passage into Yorkshire. Under the direction of Colonel John Rosworm, a German military engineer, they built earthworks, which were further fortified by the emplacement of two cannon. At

Sowerby Bridge, seven miles beyond Blackstonedge, lay the enemy, Colonel Wentworth's advanced cavalry outpost. Between the two garrisons was a no-man's-land where cavaliers and roundheads ventured at their peril.

SATURDAY, 8TH

The royalist Sir William Savile, Governor of both the City of York and Sheffield Castle, issued the following directive to his deputy-in-command at Sheffield, Major Beaumont:

> You are to send my own company and Captain Maude's company presently to Halifax, there to receive further orders from the Major General. . . . Send Sir Francis Wortley word of your march for fear you give him alarm and let the companies march presently.

With the regiments of Halifax greatly under strength, numbering in all about 1500 men, news of Captain Maude's departure from Sheffield with further reinforcements must have been welcomed by Major General Mackworth.

MONDAY, 10TH

Francis Clark of Burlington (Bridlington) was buried at Halifax, the first of many cavalier casualties.

FRIDAY, 14TH

From Halifax, we look now to Oxford. The King and his wife, Henrietta Maria, made a triumphant procession through the city to celebrate the Queen's safe return. Henrietta, having pawned the Crown Jewels abroad, had landed at Bridlington on 22 February; from there she travelled to York (the King's northern capital). Then, together with over 4000 horse and foot, a convoy of arms, supplies and money, she set out from York on 4 June and proceeded southwards through enemy territory.

In bringing these reinforcements to Oxford, the Queen greatly strengthened the royalist cause. Success for Charles seemed assured.

However, victory for King or Parliament meant nothing at all to Thomas Trotter, the second of Mackworth's soldiers to die at Halifax and whose funeral was being held this very day.

*

While the King and Queen were making merry at Oxford, 200 men from Colonel Wentworth's regiment saddled their horses and rode confidently from King Cross through Sowerby Bridge. Their intention was to engage the enemy upon Blackstonedge.

Scouts patrolling the border must have witnessed their approach and, being given passage through their own barricades, galloped down from the high moors to Littleborough, then forward to Rochdale to raise the general alarm.

Meanwhile, on the moors the first skirmish between the Yorkshire cavaliers and the Lancashire roundheads had begun.

In an attempt to break through the pass, the cavalry charged, but was met with cannon and musket fire. Soon it was sword against sword. The black peat underfoot proved treacherous for the horses; they floundered helplessly, up to their bellies in the soft earth. The attack was doomed to failure.

Some of Wentworth's soldiers were killed, others taken prisoner. Those who returned to quarters, tired and despondent, reported to their fellows 'that they will hardly have passage that way, because it is naturally so strong that five hundred men can

The Blackstonedge skirmish

keep one thousand, neither is that way fit, either for carriages or ordnance.'

No matter how Parliament might fail or falter in the rest of the kingdom, Lancashire would surely defend its Pennine frontiers against all that the enemy could offer.

In truth, the Halifax Cavaliers had not the strength of arms to mount a full offensive and decided therefore to leave the enemy in possession of its outposts, but to watch all the while for threating intentions and movements . . .

SATURDAY, 22ND

Sir Francis Mackworth to Lieutenant Colonel Wentworth at his quarters at King Cross:

> I have even now received advertisement that a party of the enemy is on foot wherefore I desire that you will take care to give notice to the horse under your command or direction to be in readiness to advance upon half an hour's warning if there be cause of which you shall have further notice.
>
> Halifax, past 6 at night.

*

Four days after Mackworth's written words to Wentworth, Prince Rupert, a gifted and dashing cavalry leader and nephew of the King, stormed Bristol, the second city of England. It was an act which demonstrated the very heights of royalist military achievements; the expectation of an early and absolute victory swept the kingdom.

Meanwhile the parliamentarians fell into despair.

To hasten the rebels' defeat, the Earl of Newcastle, not

wishing to remain idle in an all but defeated Yorkshire, campaigned anew. His advance across the county border was not into Lancashire, as expected, but Lincolnshire. There he routed all who raged against him, including cavalry under the command of the up-and-coming Colonel Oliver Cromwell.

As for that part of the Earl's army which had remained in Yorkshire to uphold his authority there, the end of July marked a return to more routine duties. The Halifax soldiers resumed guard and garrison duties, punctuated by lighter entertainment in the form of pilfering and plundering, to the increasing despair of the townsfolk, who were suffering the appalling misery of military rule.

The old beggars' litany took on a new meaning. 'From Hell, Hull and Halifax, Good Lord deliver us!' The belief in Hell was very real in the seventeenth century, while Hull was feared because of the severity of its laws against vagabonds. And Halifax, still today associated with its dreaded gibbet axe, was, in the summer of 1643, the most miserable of townships.

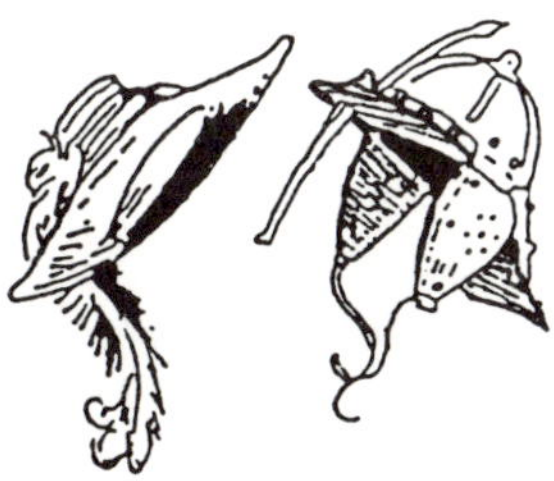

CHAPTER TWO

August 1643

Anne Tattersall of Warley Town - The Priestleys of Soyland - The King's army and its plunderings - Border fights, skirmishes and eight cavalier casualties - The Earl of Newcastle's return to Yorkshire

SUNDAY, 6TH

Anne, wife of Edmund Tattersall of Warley Town, was one of many puritans who fled into Lancashire to escape the military rule of the royalists, but, unlike the majority of Halifax exiles, Anne was never to return home, for she died at Burnley, being buried on this day.

*

Anne Green followed Anne Tattersall to a Burnley grave seven days later, and Semeon Wormald of Luddenden a month or so after Mistress Green. Many more did not survive the period of banishment.

The Yorkshire folk found a common cause in Lancashire, but to dwell there was only the lesser of two evils. Soldiers, horses, whole armies were billeted on the people, and the empty bellies and pockets of roundheads could be as burdensome as those of cavaliers. Such overcrowding and the filth that went with it soon took their toll of the elderly and the sick. Why then did Anne Tattersall and so many others flee the King's army for this deprivation?

The traditional image of a chivalrous gallant, magnificently attired in velvet cloak and hat resplendent with plumes, of young gentlemen astride white chargers who took away the ladies' breath, would have seemed strange to those who knew the reality.

The troops who marched into Halifax, Newcastle's lambs or whitecoats, so-named because of their jackets of rough undyed wool, were dirty, ill-disciplined, vengeful and feared. They originated from the Border Counties and took the King's service for eight pennies a day, wages which usually were well in arrears, so the men fully expected to supplement their lack of pay by pillaging. Food, which at times was as scarce as money, consisted for the most part of a very basic ration of bread and cheese, and anything more to the soldiers' taste had to be stolen.

This 'popish army' was feared all the more because it was thought that its ranks were rife with catholics seeking only for blood - English protestant blood.

An accurate picture of Newcastle's forces, or rather the emotions they evoked, is documented by a citizen of Bradford as he awaited their coming after the Battle of Adwalton Moor. Joseph Lister, an eyewitness, wrote of the people's terror at the time:

> Now, reader, here stop; stop for a moment; and suppose thyself to be in a like dilemma! Imagine every countenance overspread with sorrow; every house overwhelmed with grief; husbands lamenting over their families; women wringing their hands in despair; children shrieking, crying, and clinging to their parents; death in all his dreadful forms and frightful aspects, stalking in every street and every corner; in short, horror! despair!

It was to escape the 'horror and despair' dispensed by the cavaliers that Anne Tattersall and the like toiled over the high Pennine roads into Lancashire.

THURSDAY, 10TH

Unlike the Halifax townsfolk, who at least could choose to stay or go, for the citizens trapped within the walls of Gloucester no escape was possible. The King's army from Oxford and Prince Rupert's forces from Bristol (a combined total of 30,000 men) had surrounded the city and now demanded its surrender. When the people refused, the King made preparation to deal with such 'obstinate traiterly rogues'.

*

By laying siege to Gloucester, the King was unwittingly to revive Parliament's almost broken cause, for London, which was close to surrender, now rallied anew to help her sister city.

On 22 August, exactly a year to the day after the King had raised his war standard at Nottingham, the Earl of Essex, Lord General to Parliament, would march a fine and confident army out of the capital, his intention being the relief of Gloucester.

MONDAY, 14TH

But the Earl of Essex could do nothing to help the Halifax folk, for whom pillaging and lawlessness had become the order of the day. In an attempt to curb those soldiers who were beyond control, Sir Francis Mackworth issued the following command:

Forasmuch as His Excellency, the Earl of Newcastle, . . . hath by his proclamations often prohibited plundering, pillaging, and straggling of soldiers from their colours without warrant, . . . nevertheless the officers and soldiers in this army . . . have most disobediently . . . plundered and pillaged all or the most parts of the inhabitants hereabouts . . . to the utter ruin of this part of the country. These are, therefore, strictly to charge and require all officers and soldiers quartered in this vicarage and hereabouts, upon pain of death not to travel a mile from their colours, and also that they forbear at all times hereafter to take away the goods, cattle, or chattels of any person whatsoever.

*

Whether or not the General's warning was heeded is uncertain, for men who are hungry and whose pay is well in arrears are not easily disciplined.

Some families and households, because of their self-proclaimed sympathies for Parliament, would always be fair game for pillage, even in the eyes of Sir Francis. In this respect, pity the poor Priestleys of Soyland - husband, wife and sons.

Joseph Priestley was a typical yeoman of the time, living in a hillside house and combining clothmaking with farming on small plots of land. His hardy Pennine sheep produced the coarse wool which he put out to weavers, or sold to the dealers or broggers who then traded at local markets. Some of the cloth the Priestleys produced was destined for London. One of Joseph's sons, Tom, made regular journeys between Goodgreave, the family's home in Soyland (the house still stands today), and Blackwell Hall, the cloth exchange in London. The cloth, £20 worth, was carried by eight or nine strong little

Galloways; on the return trip the ponies were laden with finer wool from Kent or Suffolk.

The King's constant attempts to raise money through dubious or illegal taxes began to eat into the clothiers' profits, including Joseph Priestley's. At first they petitioned against 'illegal pressures and impositions, by which considerable sums of money have been screwed out of our purses.' But when the winds of war came, the yeoman farmers and weavers did more than merely appeal against the King's policies, they took up arms against them.

Twenty-one-year-old Samuel Priestley, another of Joseph's sons, left his apprenticeship (with Robert Hall of Boothtown) to enlist in the Fairfax army. His mother pleaded with him not to go, but Sam replied, 'If I stay at home, I can follow no employment, but be forced to hide in one hole or another, which I cannot endure. I had rather venture my life in the field, and if I die, it is in a good cause.'

So off to the wars went young Samuel, only to witness the downfall of his cause upon Adwalton Moor and the coming of the cavaliers to Halifax. Like many a fellow soldier, he retreated into Lancashire, awaiting the day when the exiled Yorkshire roundheads would re-form and return to seek revenge upon the enemy.

Joseph, now a man with a price on his head, also crossed Blackstonedge into Lancashire, as did another of his sons, Jonathan. Tom, with his intrepid train of packhorses, undaunted by the fighting all around, continued to journey to and from London, although at times he engaged a convoy to guard his goods and horses.

Mrs Priestley remained at Good-greave with her younger

The Priestleys of Good-greave, plundered and pillaged

sons, being comforted no doubt by friends and neighbours. It was not long before Mackworth's marauding men discovered her house, which lay in the midst of no-man's-land just a few miles from Sowerby Bridge. They came not once, but time and again to ransack the place, searching for the menfolk and money, and scattering her sheep across the moors. The distress and fear this must have caused Mrs Priestley was but a prelude to her calamities, for she was destined to lose far more than sheep and possessions in the months to come.

SATURDAY, 19TH

> To our very good friend Major Beaumont, of Sheffield Castle, these:
>
> We desire that you will take care that the assessment which is to be paid within Bradfield parish shall be forthwith collected for there is a necessity for the money towards payment of the soldiers. And if the goods of those that refuse to pay will not extend to make satisfaction, that you will take order that the profits of their lands may be disposed of towards payment thereof, or otherwise to apprehend their persons, if they can be found.

General Mackworth's letter was despatched only five days after his proclamation prohibiting soldiers' misdemeanours. He must have been aware that orders alone, even threats of punishment by death, could not contain the wilder spirits under his command. His men were a long way from home and family, and it was not loyalty to King Charles that kept them in a foreign county, but promises of pay or plunder.

The town's monthly assessments fell well short of the army's needs and Mackworth had little choice but to order the likes of Major Beaumont to pursue other means of funding, even adopting those methods himself. The seizure of goods, the selling of lands, or the imprisonment of persons for ransom - these procedures were designed to pay the men who would pay themselves if all else failed by ruthlessly plundering the parish.

*

Wicked acts and deeds were not merely the preserve of the royalists. Parliament had garrisoned Halifax in the first half of 1643 and the roles were then reversed, for theirs was the ravaging army. No one who supported the King was safe, not even Mr Marsh, the vicar. In May or early June he was compelled to abandon the Lord's work in Halifax and to seek instead the sanctuary of Oxford. He fled from his vicarage in the nick of time, for soldiers were sent to arrest him. They searched every corner of his house, furious to find him gone. But his wife was there, heavy with child and seriously ill.

In an uncontrollable fury, some of the roundheads stabbed their swords into the bed on which she lay, demanding to know the whereabouts of her husband. Poor Mrs Marsh was terrified to death, literally, for she went into premature labour. The newly born child, at least, survived and in the night was taken by a serving maid to a place of safety.

At times, puritans were well able to match the King's army in acts of cruelty.

SUNDAY, 27TH

'Eight others.' So reads the Halifax church registers for this day. Unnamed soldiers going to unmarked graves or a common pit.

*

Border fights, skirmishes and incursions into one another's territories, followed by casualties and the burial of the dead; these events by now were common enough.

In July, for instance, troops from the Earl of Newcastle's cavalry had ridden across the border towards Colne, only to pay dearly, for a number of men were slain and forty taken prisoner. A newspaper of the time reported: 'Accounts from travellers say that Lancashire is quiet since they beat the Newcastellians from Colne, Clitheroe and Thornton.'

The parliamentarians too risked loss of life or liberty in raiding or foraging patrols: 'The Lancashire horse still make incursions into Craven in Yorkshire, and get horses, cattle and sheep from off the lands of those against the Parliament.'

With the Earl of Newcastle now campaigning in Lincolnshire, danger threatened from that direction also: 'The King's troops at Newark had taken all the rebels' fourscore horse laden with ammunition, going from Boston to relieve all their good brethren at Manchester.'

Perhaps those eight soldiers whose deaths were recorded at Halifax were killed whilst guarding a similar convoy - horses or oxen pulling carts laden with barrels of gunpowder, or cheese and bread bound for Halifax or its satellite garrisons. Or maybe some Lancashire men from Rochdale or the Blackstonedge Garrison had entered Yorkshire in search of livestock, only to encounter stiff resistance from a company of musketeers. Giving stern reply, they may have inflicted eight deaths with pistol and sword.

Or perhaps eight lifeless troopers, slumped over horses, had

Eight cavalier casualties

been brought back to the King Cross Garrison by their comrades after a cavalry skirmish on the moors.

We will never know the truth of how those eight men met their fate, but hardly a week was to pass without others following them to the grave.

While local skirmishes were giving Francis Mackworth cause for concern, royalists occupying the East Riding found themselves with similar troubles to contend with. Hull was a safe haven to enemies of the monarch, in particular the Fairfaxes, who, though defeated at Adwalton Moor, had not been destroyed.

After the battle and a vain attempt to defend Bradford, both father and son, with the remnant of their broken army, set out towards the coast. They had several close encounters with the foe between Bradford and Hull, in one of which, at Selby, Sir Thomas Fairfax received a near-fatal wound, but eventually managed to find refuge within the walls of Hull.

Recovered from his injuries, Fairfax set about recruiting new forces - 500 foot and 700 horse - with which he raided the eastern parts of the county. These renewed attacks much alarmed the Yorkshire gentry, who eventually 'sent earnestly to my Lord of Newcastle to desire him to return [from Lincolnshire], or Yorkshire would again be lost.'

Newcastle was now faced with a dilemma. He had accomplished all he had set out to do and more. Having taken not only the greater part of Yorkshire, but Lincolnshire as well, all that remained was to march south to join the King. Together they would stab at the very heart of Parliament - London. A successful attack on the capital would virtually guarantee that the war would be over by Christmas.

But the plan to move south was deferred, for to leave the Fairfaxes in possession of Hull would be to risk the undoing of all his achievements in Yorkshire. Newcastle resolved, therefore, to continue operations in the north and to deal once and for all with the troublesome Fairfaxes.

During the last few days of August, as eight common cavaliers were being laid to rest by Mackworth's minister in Halifax, the Earl of Newcastle, with 12,000 foot, 7000 horse and 'one thousand bloody women' (camp followers) again came marching into Yorkshire.

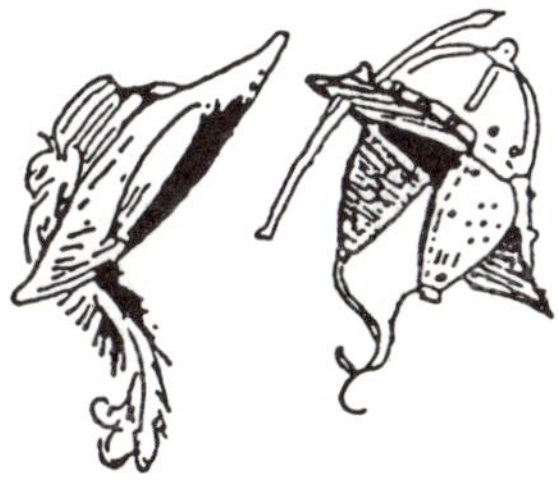

CHAPTER THREE

September 1643

The Earl of Newcastle lays siege to Hull - Mid-September scenes at Halifax - The cavalry garrison of King Cross - The capture and death of Joseph Priestley - Parliament goes on the offensive

SATURDAY, 2ND

This day, the army of the Earl of Newcastle assembled before the gates of Hull. Again the Earl opposed the Fairfaxes, and once more he had the opportunity to destroy the parliamentarians in Yorkshire. Hull must be taken, but not by storm - its walls were impregnable, nor by sea - Parliament ruled the waves. One method only might bring success. Earth forts were built, ditches dug, artillery placed in position. This was the siege of Hull.

*

As one siege began, another was drawing to its close. The Earl of Essex with his relieving force came within sight of Gloucester on 5 September, thwarting the King's plans for taking the city before the final assault on London. On the 7th, Charles was forced to withdraw his besieging army to Sudeley Castle.

The Earl of Essex entered Gloucester to fortify the garrison with supplies and ammunition, but he could not stay, for without his army London was entirely defenceless. Realizing as much, the King resolved to destroy Essex on his journey back to London, after which the capital could be taken almost at leisure.

At this critical moment, when victory for King or Parliament lay balanced on the scales, General Mackworth at Halifax was attending to more mundane matters.

SATURDAY, 9TH

Sir Francis Mackworth to Major Beaumont:

Sir, by an especial order from His Excellency (the Earl of Newcastle) these are to desire you to send me a catalogue of the names of your prisoners, with their offences for which they stand committed, and likewise the terms of their imprisonment, and as near as you can, the value of their estates both real and personal. Hereof I pray fail not - Your servant to command.

*

Busy as he was with the siege of Hull, Newcastle found time for his letters. The eternal problem of money demanded a form of stocktaking to determine the worth of all prisoners taken by General Mackworth, who, in turn, having sent the more prosperous puritans of Halifax to the dungeons of Sheffield Castle, desired the same from Major Beaumont.

Thomas Beaumont, Sir William Savile's deputy in command, governed Sheffield and its castle in much the same manner as Mackworth controlled Halifax. He too had a puritan populace to contend with. The small landowners and forgemasters (counterparts of the West Riding clothiers) combined farming with the making of cutlery and edge tools. But now the forges and furnaces of Sheffield were compelled to produce not ploughshares and the like, but swords, pike heads, cannon and musket balls, weaponry to be sent in convoy under guard to the various royalist garrisons in Yorkshire and Lincolnshire.

On one occasion an officer in command of such supplies bound for the Halifax Garrison no doubt carried the catalogue of names of prisoners which Sir Francis Mackworth and the Earl of Newcastle had requested.

THURSDAY, 14TH

At Hull Lord Fairfax ordered the sluices be opened to let in the waters from the Hull and Humber estuaries, thus flooding many of the enemy's earthworks and ditches and disrupting their siege operations.

FRIDAY, 15TH

From Gloucester the army of the Earl of Essex began its hazardous journey back to London, being stalked every inch of the way by the King's and Prince Rupert's forces awaiting an opportune moment to attack.

*

While the King opposed Essex for England's future and Newcastle vied with the Fairfaxes for the fate of Yorkshire, the Halifax Cavaliers enjoyed a calm before the storm. As summer gave way to autumn, they could not know that five weeks hence they too would be embroiled in bitter conflict against a foe sent from Lancashire directly to oppose them.

Meanwhile, the military occupation of this West Riding town inexorably altered its appearance and character.

A few years before the war Halifax had been described as 'a pretty well-built town of stone, consisting much of clothiers. . . . Here is one of the fairest inns in England called ye Cross. . . . Kept by a widow woman.' The widow woman's ale was, no doubt, reserved now for General Mackworth, high-ranking officers and the royalist gentry, while the common rabble got not so much as a look in.

Halifax was no longer pretty. Its narrow streets were littered with straw, dung and filth, causing sickness among the soldiers and citizens alike. Draught horses constantly moved military supplies and baggage wagons through the town, while Wentworth's cavalry herded pillaged livestock into pens. On market days, local farmers had the opportunity of buying back their own animals.

The town was noisy with drinking, cursing, belligerent soldiers, while those on duty with little else to do were drilled by officers on open ground.

Pikemen wielded steel-tipped pikes made from stout ash poles up to 18 feet long. They wore iron helmets, leather buff coats, back and breast armour, and a sword.

Musketeers regularly practised volley firing. The men were divided into lines, one kneeling, the others stooping or standing. After firing, the lines would change places, go through the lengthy procedure of reloading, then fire again. Each musketeer carried a dozen accurate measures of gunpowder, in addition to musket balls, wads and fine priming powder.

In fields and enclosures around King Cross, Wentworth's cavalry, the elite troops of the Halifax army, performed their manoeuvres. A cavalryman's weapons included a basket-hilt sword, two flintlock pistols and occasionally a flintlock carbine. Little armour was worn, for men and horses could

Halifax Cavaliers

move more swiftly when unimpeded by too much weight.

In and around the town Halifax regiments marched to the beat of drum behind their colours, flags which were used for identification or as a rallying point in the midst of battle. High on the hills, at the vantage points of Sentry Edge and Roils Head, these proudly erected colours billowed, denoting the company guarding the outpost.

As General Mackworth's soldiers were being drilled and disciplined, the town's dignitaries attempted to uphold some semblance of civil order. The township had to be strictly controlled so that sufficient goods and food were produced to enable the occupying army to be fed and maintained. If this were to fail because of stealing and looting, sources of food and income would cease. Ironically, were this to happen, the cavaliers would become increasingly unruly, resulting in yet more orders from the General to try to stem their plunderings.

At least the parish was quieter on Sundays. This day brought a temporary truce between soldiers and civilians, who uneasily joined together in the worship of the Lord.

Sir Francis Mackworth, his royalist officers and staff, hats removed, would enter Halifax Church (a fifteenth-century building dedicated to the patron saint of clothiers - St John the Baptist), for a divine service acceptable to His Majesty. Puritan parishioners, with black hats firmly placed upon heads, would lodge in opposite pews, gritting teeth and suppressing anger at having to sit through sermons and ceremonies not at all to their liking. Gone were the joyful days when they were free to listen to the likes of Mr Elkanah Wales, a fire and brimstone preacher who would often 'spend six or seven hours in prayer and preaching, and rarely go out of the pulpit.'

WEDNESDAY, 20TH

The race and chase to London by Essex and the King came to its conclusion this day, when Charles finally caught his quarry at Newbury. But a final conflict it was not to be, for Essex's army, essential for the defence of London, was not destroyed. After twelve hours of fighting, with gunpowder almost exhausted, the royalists were compelled to withdraw to headquarters at Oxford.

*

Five days after the battle, on 25 September, 'the Earl of Essex was received in London with all imaginable demonstrations of affection and reverence.' With his army intact and London saved, the scales began to tip in favour of Parliament.

Had the Battle of Newbury gone the King's way, the war would have been over, but now, far from being finished, the war widened by enveloping other nations.

On the day the Earl of Essex began his march back to London from Gloucester, the King concluded military negotiations with the Irish; then, as Essex re-entered the capital, Parliament formed its own alliance with Scotland. However, it would be some time before Irish troops could land to assist the cavaliers and before the Scots crossed the English border to fight for the roundheads.

Both King and Parliament now knew that this 'war without an enemy' was also a war with no immediate end in sight.

WEDNEDAY, 27TH

The great siege of Hull continued to claim its casualties. Few civilians and soldiers were killed. Instead, horses were the victims. The newly raised cavalry troops of Sir Thomas Fairfax, now confined within the walls of Hull, became quite useless, for there was no food or grazing to maintain the horses 'and many died every day, having nothing but salt water about the town.' This day, therefore, Sir Thomas, with most of his horse and dragoons, took ship across the Humber estuary for Lincolnshire, where, upon landing, they were met by Colonel Cromwell. Lord Fairfax, now Governor of Hull, remained behind to continue the confrontation with Newcastle.

*

By now, military operations in the Halifax area consisted of little more than the usual theft of horses, sheep and cattle - villainies perpetrated mainly by Wentworth's cavalrymen.

With over 400 horses and men to contend with, the villagers and farmers of King Cross found themselves extremely hard pressed. Colonel Wentworth's own quarters there would have been at 'the best house', from which he could command the garrison, make study of maps to determine the lie of the land, and generally issue his orders. His officers lodged nearby in accommodation suitable to their rank, while common troopers were assigned to various billets, in the homes of the poor, farms, barns, or under rough tentage in the main camp.

The hundreds of grazing horses were guarded day and night by sentinels, although each man was responsible for the welfare of his own animal, 'for if a soldier by negligence or malice hurt his horse, or use him so ill that he die; he shall not only bear the loss of him, but be chastised by his superiors, and be chased from the company.' Wentworth's officers implemented these directions as set out in John Cruso's *Military Instructions for the Cavalry*, a soldiers' manual published in 1632.

All approaches to King Cross were guarded and blocked by felled trees, or posts and chains. Protected within these 'barracadoes' was the baggage train - wagons containing the officers' personal belongings along with regimental weaponry and armoury. There were also the sutlers' or victuallers' carts from which were issued the soldiers' rations. At the raising of a general alarm, musketeers or dragoons would encircle the baggage to defend these precious commodities.

Each morning the men received a rude awakening by officers, who, as Cruso states, 'not giving ear to the murmering of the soldiers would go from house to house, knocking and calling to the men, causing them to saddle their horses and to see them armed and ready to mount, punishing those that are sluggish.' So would begin another day of patrols, raids and, at times, skirmishes.

When engaged upon foraging duties, for mutual protection the King Cross cavalry combined with the Halifax infantry. Such a convoy, with empty carts and wagons, would go in search of sustenance for the army, 'issuing out to Honley, Holmfirth, Marsden and Saddleworth'. Having loaded their wagons with food and plunder, the soldiers commenced a retreat to quarters. The poor condition of many roads, particularly in wet weather when deep mud impeded passage, made these slow-moving convoys a fine target for the Lancashire roundheads.

So, to deter their enemies from entering Yorkshire or simply as a show of strength, troops of horse were sent from King Cross to patrol the county border, as Joseph Priestley, the exiled yeoman, found to his cost.

The capture of Joseph Priestley, the yeoman

One day he left the safety of Lancashire intending a final farewell with his wife at Good-greave before going to London to see what was left of the cloth trade there. Leading his horse through the soldiers' encampment at Blackstonedge, Joseph must have received warning that, once through the barricades he would be unprotected and within reach of the enemy.

Yet still he resolved to undertake the hazardous five-mile trek to his home. As a thick mist lay heavy on the hills, all that was visible were the few yards of moorland track before him.

A mile or so into his journey, he halted and listened intently, as from the distance came the clatter of hooves and the rattle of armour. Out of the gloom appeared a troop from Wentworth's cavalry. They immediately seized Joseph and conveyed him to Halifax, where 'he was made prisoner with some others of like quality at the corner house in Southgate.' Refusing to pay the price of his freedom, a ransom of £80, he was kept under house arrest. Never one for self-pity, he spent the long days comforting his fellow captives with scripture readings, hymns and prayers, to the amusement of the cavaliers who called the prisoners 'puritans and roundheads'.

Mrs Priestley, in an effort to ease her husband's sufferings, sent him 'bedding, clean linen and money, and whatever he stood in need of every week.' Even so, it was not long before Joseph fell sick, for being an active man he found it very difficult to contend with close confinement.

Eventually General Mackworth agreed to Joseph's removal to the house of John Brearcliffe, the apothecary, who still remained in Lancashire.

Perhaps Tom Priestley should end the old yeoman's story.

> My father had the liberty of [Brearcliffe's] house and was attended by

his own servant and a neighbour woman to us at Good-greave. In a few days it pleased God to take him to himself. He was interred behind the font in Halifax Church as decently as was possible for a man in his circumstances, and as the calamity of those times would permit.

Without any in Yorkshire to oppose them, the King's army had inflicted upon many puritans miseries similar to those endured by the Priestleys. But events were now beginning to move rapidly against the royalists, both locally and nationally.

To march against London the King required the strength of his northern forces, but the Earl of Newcastle remained stubbornly in Yorkshire, maintaining the siege of Hull.

In Lincolnshire, Sir Thomas Fairfax, 'Black Tom' as he was nick-named, and Oliver Cromwell, 'Old Noll', campaigned together in an attempt to destroy the effects of Newcastle's occupation in that county and to restore its parliamentarians' will to fight on.

This growing optimism extended into Lancashire and began to stiffen the resolve of the Yorkshiremen there. As October approached, many of these exiles living in or around Manchester began to talk of a new offensive in Yorkshire, so that an air of expectancy developed in these so-recently beaten and banished men.

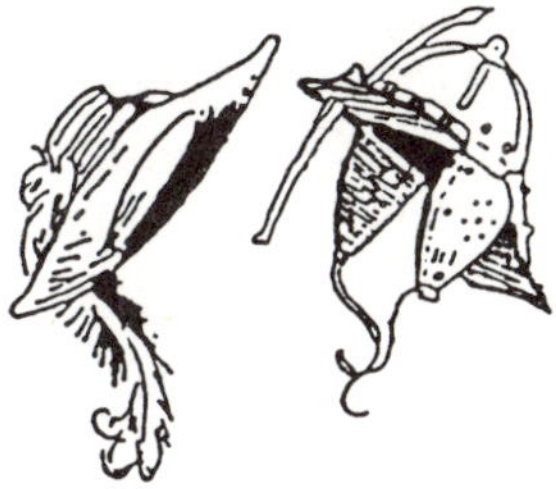

CHAPTER FOUR

October 1643

The conclusion of the Siege of Hull and the Battle of Winceby - Colonel Bradshaw agrees to lead the Yorkshiremen - A general muster at Rochdale - Colonel Bradshaw enters Heptonstall - Sowerby occupied - The attack on Hollins House - Sir Francis Mackworth prepares for reprisals

SUNDAY, 1ST

Colonel Huddlestone, one of General Mackworth's officers, must have wished that he had not a month or so earlier departed Yorkshire for Cumberland. Leaving his regiment at Halifax and collecting a force of 1600 men in Furness, he marched to the relief of Thurland Castle. The castle, situated thirteen miles to the northeast of Lancaster, was one of the King's three remaining strongholds in Lancashire, but even it was now under siege. Without waiting to be attacked, the besiegers, commanded by Colonel Rigby, intercepted their adversaries at Lindale, near the Lancashire-Cumberland border.

In a battle lasting only fifteen minutes the royalists were scattered in confusion. Few were killed, but the parliamentary cavalry, in pursuit, captured two captains, an ensign, 400 men, an ammunition train and Colonel Huddlestone.

*

In Yorkshire, at Hull, as the month progressed and despite 'many fiery hot bullets being shot into the town day and night' (red-hot cannon balls), the defenders were gaining more and more confidence in their ability to withstand the siege.

At Horncastle in Lincolnshire the armies of Cromwell and Fairfax continued to grow in strength and numbers, forcing 2800 horse and dragoons under Sir John Henderson to march out of Newark in an attempt to oppose them.

Simultaneously in both counties a drama was unfolding in which the Earl of Newcastle's impressive military achievements were to receive a serious setback.

WEDNESDAY, 11TH

At Winceby, near Horncastle, a great cavalry conflict was fought in which Oliver Cromwell led the charge against the Newark cavaliers. Despite his horse being shot from under him, his disciplined troops pressed home the attack and broke the enemy's lines. A second charge, commanded by Sir Thomas Fairfax, completed the rout, after which, as the Earl of Manchester (commander-in-chief of the Eastern Association) tells us, 'our men had little else to do but pursue a flying enemy, which they did for many miles.'

Returning from the chase, the roundheads heard the sound of distant cannon fire. Coincidentally, Lord Fairfax at Hull had also taken the offensive. Fifteen hundred foot and four troops of horse, under the immediate command of Sir John Meldrum, had thrown open the gates and sallied forth to attack the enemy's works and trenches. As Newcastle's men fled, their own guns were turned and fired upon them, the sound of which was heard over forty miles away at Winceby.

In the evening, as the Earl of Newcastle made preparations to retrieve the guns and ground which had been lost around Hull, a messenger arrived with news of the defeat at Winceby. The Earl held a council of war to determine the course of action to be taken now that the fall of Lincolnshire threatened.

THURSDAY, 12TH

After six long weeks, in the early hours the siege of Hull was raised. Newcastle could no longer remain there while his enemies rampaged unchecked in the Midlands. Part of his army, therefore, went into Lincolnshire to deal with Cromwell and Fairfax; the rest marched away to York to maintain control of Yorkshire.

*

News of the Battle of Winceby, the ending of the siege of Hull and the movements of Newcastle's army - all were of the greatest strategic importance for both sides.

Intelligence of these events was relayed by messengers or 'posts' riding swift horses. All day and through the night, galloping from garrison to garrison, they carried the news through each county.

It was not long before these couriers rode into Lancashire, making for the parliamentarians' stronghold at Manchester, not only to deliver the necessary information there, but also, albeit unwittingly, to initiate the next episode in the Halifax and Heptonstall story.

The full significance of the royalist double defeat must have been well understood by the Manchester soldiers, but particularly by all Yorkshiremen in the town. From being master of two counties, the Earl of Newcastle was now commanding in hostile territory.

Perhaps three or four Halifax men, weary of their long exile in Lancashire, thought that it was high time Sir Francis Mackworth was reduced to the same predicament in which Newcastle now found himself. Over flagons of ale in a Manchester tavern they discussed ways in which the Halifax Garrison could be demoralized or weakened.

SATURDAY, 14TH

Their embryonic plots grew, as a deputation presented the Manchester high command with an appeal for leadership and organization. The men requested the formation of an army which would enter Yorkshire, specifically to oppose the Halifax Cavaliers. Heptonstall, a hill-top village ten miles to the west of Halifax (by way of the old roads) would serve well as a base from which to commence a localized campaign.

Colonel Robert Bradshaw, a Manchester officer, thought well of the plan and agreed to command the bold venture. He sent out notices of intent to ministers in outlying towns, for in those days churches were used not only for worship, but as meeting places where news was exchanged. The many Yorkshire refugees who lay idle and inactive in East Lancashire and who were to attend church service on the morrow would welcome indeed a general call to arms.

SUNDAY, 15TH

In sixteen churches and chapels puritan preachers proclaimed

Colonel Bradshaw agrees to lead the Yorkshiremen

the word and then urged the men into battle. Congregations listened intently, as from pulpits so-called 'Godly ministers' mingled religious reflections with politics and news of the war - Hull was saved and Fairfax victorious at Winceby. Surely this was the hand and providence of God against those who opposed Parliament.

Now from Manchester came news of an intended offensive against the enemy closer to home. All those willing to cross the Pennine hills to fight in the West Riding (this was to be a voluntary force) must report presently to the garrison at Rochdale, to be listed for military service.

TUESDAY, 17TH

Responding to the call, from all surrounding areas the Yorkshiremen came to attend the general muster. Rochdale was already burdened with 1200 soldiers and now hundreds more converged on the town, which was a convenient gathering place, the last stronghold in Lancashire from which an army could begin its advance into Yorkshire. Communications and regular convoys carrying ammunition, food and soldiers' pay were essential. Rochdale would supply those needs.

This day, therefore, and the next, Colonel Bradshaw with the town's dignitaries pondered the many difficulties and logistical problems of maintaining an army garrisoned in enemy territory.

THURSDAY, 19TH

Marching out of Rochdale on both this and the following day, gallant, if small and ill-equipped, bands of men gathered at

Heptonstall and there prepared to make a stand for Parliament.

Colonel Bradshaw's army consisted of one troop of horse (about sixty men), some 280 musketeers and 500 'clubmen', irregular soldiers and volunteers armed with whatever weapons came to hand, which often amounted to little more than various farming tools or clubs and cudgels.

Bradshaw's second-in-command was Major Eden. They were assisted by two Yorkshire captains, Farrer and Taylor, and a Lancashire officer, Captain Helliwell.

Among the common ranks was Samuel Priestley. With his father dead, his mother distraught, Good-greave plundered and his trade in ruins, he surely had just reason for seeking revenge on those responsible for his and his family's misfortunes. Also present was John Brearcliffe, who, having said farewell to his new-found Lancashire wife Dorothy, offered his services as surgeon.

Over the hills and as yet unaware of the Heptonstall Roundheads lay the enemy, the Halifax Cavaliers. In order to wage war on them, Colonel Bradshaw, who was a stranger to the locality, relied on those Yorkshiremen with knowledge of the packhorse trails and drovers' tracks across the difficult country between Heptonstall and Halifax. Local well-wishers also came forward with valuable information about Mackworth's headquarters, as well as his outer garrisons. Armed with such intelligence, on the following morning the Heptonstall commander began his campaign.

SATURDAY, 21ST

Using stealth to prevent his approach being observed, Colonel Bradshaw marched a force from Heptonstall over Hathershelf to occupy Sowerby, a township perilously close to Wentworth's advanced outpost. From this vantage point Bradshaw could witness for himself the comings and goings of the enemy at Sowerby Bridge and King Cross, while at the same time studying the lie of the land for the the military operations to come.

*

The occupation of Sowerby continued for two days. During this time musket fire was exchanged and the Heptonstall soldiers appear to have captured men, arms and horses. Nevertheless, General Mackworth gave orders for his army to remain strictly on the defensive until the strength and intentions of the enemy could the better be determined.

It could only be a matter of time, however, before the King Cross cavalry rode through Sowerby Bridge and up the steep hill to attack in force. Bradshaw knew as much and presently marched his men away, but continued his tactics of harassing and alarming the royalists.

MONDAY, 23RD

From Sowerby, Colonel Bradshaw, Captain Taylor and two Lancashire companies began the short march across the old Roman ford at Longbottom, along the hillside and up through Hollins Wood in the township of Warley, until they reached Hollins House (formerly called Murgatroyd). This imposing structure had been rebuilt only ten years previously by James and Mary Murgatroyd.

James Murgatroyd was a wealthy man whose fortune had

largely been made in the woollen trade. Unlike most other West Riding clothiers, he was a King's man. He had built many fine houses in the area and he put The Hollins at the disposal of Sir Francis Mackworth, who in turn stored arms and ammunition there. Colonel Bradshaw, acting on good reconnaissance, learned that these supplies were in all probability bound for the nearby outposts of Roils Head and Sentry Edge. He had other plans for them.

The secluded house was guarded by a small force of some fifty or so men under the command of a captain and an ensign. At the first indication of the enemy's approach the defenders barricaded themselves in.

The attacking force surrounded the house and attempted to gain entrance; yet despite the battering it received, the strong oak door stubbornly held fast. Attention was soon diverted to the windows, but these were so narrow that not even the smallest of Bradshaw's men could get his shoulders through.

When the roundheads began to hack away at one of the stone mullions, the besieged retreated to the upper rooms. Some of them climbed onto the roof and, perching uneasily on the housetop, ripped out and hurled stone slates at the attackers, yet injured only one man.

The cavaliers fought valiantly for about an hour, but when at last the mullion gave way and the house was entered, further resistance became futile and the garrison surrendered. Not all the men were captured, for amidst the confusion the captain, leaving his command to the ensign, managed to reach his horse and was seen to gallop off in the direction of Halifax. Three others escaped the net and, although on foot, quickly reached the nearby outpost of Roils Head or Sentry Edge. It was

The attack on Hollins House

essential for the attackers to make an immediate withdrawal before the inevitable arrival of reinforcements.

With the prize of a plentiful supply of much-needed arms and gunpowder, and forty-four prisoners including the ensign, Colonel Bradshaw completed his successful three-day campaign by returning safely to Heptonstall.

At Halifax, General Mackworth, in less buoyant mood, listened intently as a bedraggled and weary captain gave his account of the attack on Hollins House.

*

Negligence, disorganization, demoralization owing to insufficient food and pay must all have contributed to the lack of success for the Halifax army in the skirmishes at Sowerby and Warley.

In order to restore the morale of his troops and regain the upper hand, Mackworth, having now intelligence of the enemy's main camp, resolved to attack them in force, to clear them out of Yorkshire with one decisive blow.

Well aware of the certainty of reprisals, Colonel Bradshaw set his men to fortifying and strengthening the Heptonstall defences. Barricades shielded the village; great stones and boulders were placed at vantage points, ready to be levered and rolled down the steep hillside upon an advancing enemy; and companies of musketeers patrolled the wooded precipice which surrounded the settlement and its adjacent fields. All the while, guards on top of the old church tower scanned the valley and the hills, watching and waiting for the approach of danger.

SUNDAY, 29TH

'Sore streaming in the night, being all the night as light as moonlight.'

So reported those Heptonstall guards standing on duty in the cold dark hours after witnessing an impressive display of shooting stars.

Their royalist foe at Halifax must also have beheld the heavenly entertainment. Perhaps Sir Francis Mackworth, having finalized his plans for an attack on Heptonstall, now looked towards the skies and became filled with foreboding. In an age when people told the time from the movement of the sun, and the phases of the moon foretold when the darkest nights would fall, when travel was best avoided, conjunctions of planets, eclipses and the arrival of comets or shooting stars were seen as signs of war, doom or disaster . . .

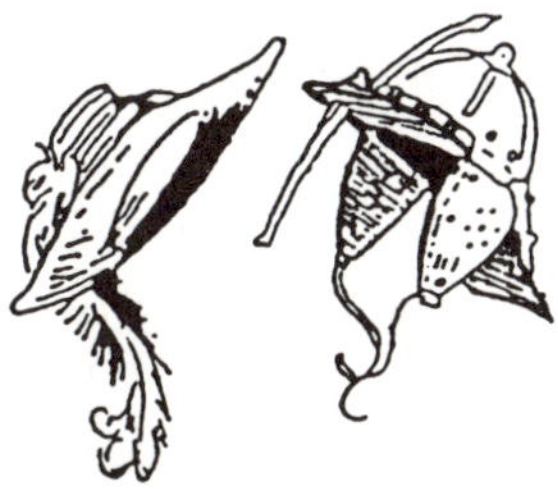

CHAPTER FIVE

November 1643

The Battle of Heptonstall - The Irish landings - The upkeep and maintenance of Colonel Bradshaw's army - Heptonstall in peace and war - The Scottish alliance concluded - The death of Samuel Priestley

WEDNESDAY, 1ST

Halifax; three in the morning or thereabouts.

In the cold and the dark, a shivering army of 400 cavalrymen and 400 musketeers prepared to march out of the town. As the order was given, the large column moved westwards towards the gibbet axe (a guillotine used to execute thieves who had stolen cloth above the value of 13 pence from tenterhooks), then steadily uphill to Highroad Well and Newlands. From Luddenden the long stream of marching soldiers continued straight up the opposite hillside, through Midgley Town and along the windswept moorland road to Mount Skip, eventually dropping into the valley below.

Having travailed the main road between Halifax and Heptonstall, the royalist army gathered at the river's edge at Hebden Bridge. On the other side of the old humpbacked bridge was the Buttress, the steep medieval packhorse track which climbed the hill towards Heptonstall. Here Colonel Bradshaw, having intelligence of the enemy's approach, had instructed his men to take up their positions, a manoeuvre which repeated practice had perfected.

As dawn broke, blustering winds and driving rain began to hinder the attacking force. The musketeers in particular were vulnerable to the adverse weather because they relied upon a smouldering cord to ignite dry gunpowder for firing their muskets. Having crossed the bridge, troops of horse and companies of foot soldiers began to scale the precipitous hillside towards Heptonstall over 500 feet above them.

Without warning, great rocks, dislodged by the defenders, came crashing down the hill. Many of the first casualties of the battle were crushed beneath boulders and flailing hooves.

Notwithstanding this assault and stinging fire from the Heptonstall musketeers, who despite the torrential rain had kept their powder dry, the cavaliers continued to advance, but only until the roundheads sallied forth from the village.

Difficult as the terrain was, there followed a fierce and bitter combat at close quarters. Numbers were more or less equal, though the attacking force was overwhelmingly superior in cavalry. But a more unsuitable place in which to manoeuvre horses could hardly be imagined.

Whatever tactics Colonel Bradshaw, Major Eden and Captains Farrer, Taylor and Helliwell employed on that muddy rain-drenched hillside, their ill-equipped army successfully bore down upon those below, until eventually the enemy wavered, gave ground, then broke in complete disorder. Bradshaw's men pressed home the counter-attack; exhausted, many of their opponents were killed after being driven backwards over a ridge. Musketeers on the Buttress road were trampled underfoot by their own cavalry as panic-stricken horses were spurred on by desperate riders attempting to re-cross the river.

Perhaps when they saw their antagonists falling back in

The Battle of Heptonstall

disarray, the cautious puritan inhabitants of Heptonstall seized what weapons they could lay hands on and joined Bradshaw in the chaotic scramble down the hillside. The main body of Mackworth's army, now on the low ground by the river, saw the angry crowd surging towards them. Some cavaliers, without waiting for the mass of horses and men to clear the bridge, plunged into the River Hebden, only to be swept away and drowned, for the heavy rain had turned the stream into a raging torrent.

In the midst of the confusion, there took place an act of compassion. Samuel Priestley spied an enemy soldier in the river, wounded and in danger of drowning. For a fleeting moment Samuel may have wished the man ill, remembering the death of his father, Joseph. But any vengeful thoughts were short-lived, for Sam leapt into the swollen river, caught hold of the man and dragged him to the water's edge, saving his life.

The royal army, now in full retreat, was fiercely pursued for nearly five miles along the route it had marched only hours before. With great difficulty officers in the rearguard attempted to maintain some semblance of order as a hundred musketeers and fifty horse followed doggedly at their heels; yet no lives were lost in the chase and only one of Bradshaw's men was wounded, by a sword-cut in the arm. At Luddenden village the pursuers disengaged and returned triumphantly to Heptonstall, leaving a demoralized foe to continue on to Halifax.

Meanwhile at Hebden Bridge, the aftermath of battle: A fulling mill owned by Matthew Sutcliffe, a kersey maker, was totally destroyed, presumably fired in retribution by the retreating army. There, in more peaceful times, cloth had been cleansed and thickened on primitive machines powered by a

Samuel Priestley's act of compassion

water wheel. Now, near the mill and on both sides of the river, lay royalist dead and injured.

Those who had been captured - Colonel Haukes, Captain Flood, Captain Bird, a lieutenant, a cornet and thirty-five men, some with serious injuries - were taken to Heptonstall. Locked in the old church, they awaited an armed guard to escort them to Rochdale where they would join those other unfortunates taken prisoner a week earlier at Hollins House.

Few, if any, of the defenders were killed, but a good many received wounds, including, it is believed, Colonel Bradshaw.

Samuel Priestley, despite his drenching in the river, stood guard duty that same night, only to catch a severe cold for his pains. Other roundhead soldiers, huddled around camp fires, congratulated themselves upon a considerable and well-deserved success.

At Halifax, as stragglers from the battle continued to come in, throughout the army an angry gloom prevailed. The men, strangers to the area, had little realized how impregnable the hill would prove to be, especially in such appalling weather. In addition, Sir Francis Mackworth had not anticipated such stubborn resistance.

Whatever the reasons for the failure of the attack, the end results remained the same: the Halifax Cavaliers no longer held undisputed sway over the district, while Colonel Bradshaw's army could continue its hostile tactics, but with greater resolution, having collected all the honours at the Battle of Heptonstall.

*

Eight days after the major engagement between Mackworth

and Bradshaw, Sir William Brereton's parliamentary forces, raiding from Cheshire, occupied Wrexham in North Wales, a point from which they hoped to intercept the King's Irish troops.

News of the impending arrival of reinforcements from Ireland rapidly revived the hopes of the defeated Lancashire royalists. They secured the King's warrant, enabling the 5000-strong Irish army to march to the relief of their county. New Lancashire regiments were also to be raised and help was expected from the Earl of Newcastle in Yorkshire.

Not only was Lancashire in danger of falling into the King's hands, Cheshire too was now vulnerable. If both counties were reduced to the same extremes as Yorkshire and Lincolnshire, it would do inestimable damage to the parliamentary cause. The imminent invasion by Parliament's Scottish allies would amount to little if royalist domination of the North was achieved.

Fully aware of this, the Manchester Garrison prepared for conflict as defiantly as in July, five months previously, when Newcastle had demanded its surrender. When danger had threatened from Yorkshire, Manchester had sent out men and arms to the county border. Now that an attack appeared unlikely from that quarter, supplies and resources, urgently needed elsewhere, could hardly continue being sent to Rochdale and Blackstonedge, let alone an isolated little outpost such as Heptonstall.

Yet without provisions from Lancashire, Colonel Bradshaw would be hard-pressed to continue his campaign. The untamed moorlands and marshy, overgrown, sparsely populated valleys offered little in the way of sustenance for his army.

Perhaps Cross-stone and Mankinholes came to Bradshaw's assistance. In better times, these and other villages and small settlements on the Lancashire-Yorkshire border had been home to a prosperous class of people, the yeoman families, who worked hard yet lived plainly. The only extravagance they allowed themselves was the building of fine houses, many of which are still standing. All other profits were put back into the cloth business. But with bitter resentment at the loss of trade, these proud puritans may willingly have provided goods and money for any who opposed the King's army at Halifax.

More reluctant donations towards the upkeep of the Heptonstall Garrison came from those local gentry who adhered to the royal cause. Their homes and property were plundered and pillaged by Bradshaw's raiding roundheads, in much the same manner as Mackworth's cavaliers still continued to steal from their civilian opponents.

The burden of maintaining an offensive inevitably fell largely upon the Heptonstall people, who lived, not in a sleepy village, but a large settlement, a focal point for merchants and business transactions. The surrounding area looked to Heptonstall as an important trading centre, and as a result the township, at least before the war, had thrived.

Families such as the Bentleys had become very affluent, and the Greenwoods had even risen from yeomen to the lesser gentry. Their family home, Greenwood Lee, still stands by the Widdop Road which leads directly from Heptonstall to Colne in Lancashire.

In more humble houses along the main road through Heptonstall and scattered round about lived weavers who, to supplement meagre wages, worked the land in two large open communal fields at the top end of the village. But their farming activities were only marginal, for the infertile ground, 900 feet above sea level, could not support profitable agriculture.

The main source of income came from the making of pieces of coarse woollen cloth called kersey, 18 yards long and a yard wide. This was very much a home industry, undertaken by all the family. Rows of mullioned windows, designed to let in as much light as possible, enabled work on the looms to be continued until dusk.

A household took about two weeks to complete a piece, which was then sold to dealers at the Cloth Hall on Towngate, the main road through Heptonstall. The cloth had still to undergo other processes such as dyeing, tentering and shearing, and it was at this point that fullers like Matthew Sutcliffe, the Hebden Bridge mill owner, intervened to buy and then 'finish' the cloth.

From the Cloth Hall this valuable commodity was carried on trains of strong packhorses, which could easily negotiate the Buttress road and other steep gradients encountered along the many stone causeways.

Having sold the cloth, the Heptonstall weavers bought more wool. Yet before repeating the long and arduous process, they undoubtedly sought respite in the taverns and ale houses. Drunkards, however, would evoke, if not the wrath of God, at least the anger of the churchwardens, who had the authority to submit troublemakers to the stone stocks for punishment and ridicule. Or perhaps, more appropriate for the crime, they would spend an uncomfortable and sobering night in the tiny windowless dungeon beneath Elizabethan Cottage, now known as Stag Cottage.

Come the Lord's day parishioners gathered at the medieval Church of St Thomas à Becket. Throughout his sermon the preacher, Robert Gilbodie, would cast an accusing eye and remonstrate against transgressers.

On weekdays fifty youngsters listened to similar puritanical teachings in the small classroom of the newly built grammar school. Frightening explorations of the village dungeon may have been made by the schoolchildren, or perhaps a playful turn in the stocks, to impress upon young minds the penalties for misdeeds.

In November 1643 such peaceful activities were all but forgotten. The minister had more to contend with than a wayward congregation. His church was undoubtedly used as either a temporary prison or a storehouse where arms and barrels of gunpowder could safely be kept under lock and key. The church tower served as a watchtower, while its bells, which had once called the godly to worship, now tolled only when danger threatened or as a general call to arms.

The main encampment for the occupying army was situated in the communal fields, so that soldiers and horses trampled underfoot what few crops the infertile earth had yielded. Weavers' looms were still and silent and the doors of the Cloth Hall remained firmly bolted.

Heptonstall was no longer a bustling, prosperous community, yet its citizens were determined to hold their own, in readiness for better days. As well as they were able, they contributed in cash or kind towards the furtherance of Colonel Bradshaw's campaign.

THURSDAY, 23RD

Assistance for Parliament's war efforts nationally came with the conclusion of the Scottish alliance in Edinburgh. In return for the reform of the English Church, bringing it more in line with their own, Scotland agreed to send a 20,000-strong army into England, to oppose the King and counterbalance the Irish threat.

*

Whichever side eventually won the war, or whatever the outcome of the localized struggle between Sir Francis Mackworth and Colonel Bradshaw, it mattered little to Mrs Priestley, who, towards the end of November, was to receive yet more sorrow in her already devastated life.

Still suffering from the effects of his immersion in the River Hebden, Samuel Priestley had returned to his mother at Good-greave. When his condition began to worsen, he was taken to Lancashire for medical treatment. As Jonathan Priestley tells us:

> My brother Sam went to Heptonstall . . . under the command of Colonel Bradshaw. . . . The King's army from Halifax came against the town and was beaten back. . . . Brother Sam in the pursuit saw a wounded man in the water, ready to be drowned; being an object of pity, he went into the water in his boots and drew him to dry land; he being on guard or some other necessary service, had his boots on all night, got cold, came home and fell, I think, into a fever and died in about three weeks after.

Samuel Priestley died at Rochdale and was buried there on 25 November.

November 1643

Mrs Priestley, having endured the death of her husband and son and the repeated pillaging of her home, packed what few belongings she still possessed and, along with the younger boys, left for Lancashire.

This 'unhappy war' was to be responsible for the destruction of thousands of formerly contented and prosperous families, the Priestleys of Soyland being one of many.

Tragic as Sam's death appeared, in the month that followed the Heptonstall army was to suffer a far more significant loss. And simultaneously the parliamentary leadership in London would also receive a crippling blow.

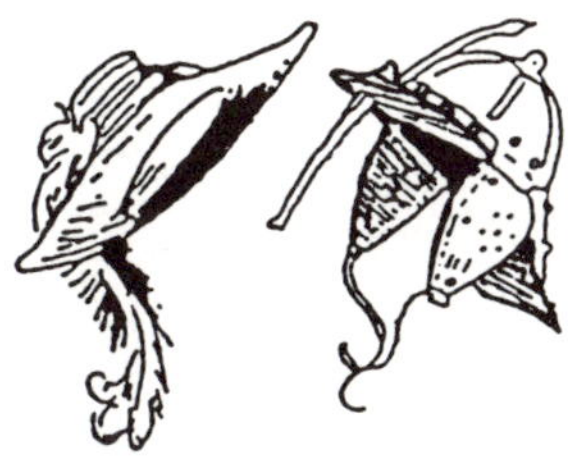

CHAPTER SIX

December 1643

The death of Colonel Bradshaw - Two cavalier deserters - The Irish army begins its offensive - Heptonstall burials - Routine activities of the Heptonstall Roundheads - Christmas day at Halifax - The Siege of Nantwich - From Lincolnshire Sir Thomas Fairfax marches into Lancashire - Major Eden prepares to attack in force

FRIDAY, 8TH

Colonel Bradshaw died 8th December: 1643   9 clock morning

So wrote John Brearcliffe as he related the death of Colonel Robert Bradshaw, the result of wounds sustained during the Battle of Heptonstall.

Brearcliffe's few words fail to convey the tragedy of the situation, but from them it is not difficult to reconstruct what must have been a sad and sorrowful scene. We may imagine a bed-ridden Bradshaw, who, in the five weeks preceding his death, despite his deteriorating condition continued to command the garrison from his sickbed.

A deeply religious man, it is more than likely that in those final hours he was comforted by the prayers of the Heptonstall minister. Also by the bedside was Brearcliffe, whose skills as a surgeon had not proved sufficient to heal his commander. Standing alongside, grim-faced and solemn, was Major Eden and the army's three captains.

At nine o'clock, when the end came, word went from the

The death of Colonel Bradshaw

sickroom to the soldiers' encampment. Maybe the church bells tolled as a melancholy mood spread throughout the village. A campaign which had culminated in a fine victory now counted little, for, with the death of Colonel Bradshaw, the prize of military success had been dearly bought.

In London, at seven in the evening, the life of the great parliamentarian, John Pym, also came to its end. His death at this critical juncture, when his negotiating skills were most needed to maintain the alliance with Scotland, was regarded as a great calamity by all Parliament men. Scottish assistance was essential, for without it defeat still threatened.

*

Despite their loss of leadership, both the Parliament's cause and the Heptonstall campaign continued on their courses. History records Oliver Cromwell as being the eventual successor to John Pym, while, according to John Brearcliffe, Colonel Bradshaw's command devolved upon Major Eden, a very capable officer as his future actions were to testify.

One of his first acts as commanding officer may have been to decide upon the credibility of statements made by two cavalier horsemen. One day, or more likely well into the night, Heptonstall sentinels had apprehended, disarmed and escorted them to headquarters for questioning. The men claimed to be deserters from the Wentworth Garrison, wishing to switch allegiance.

They must have undergone a thorough interrogation to determine the truth of their tale, for their captors would suspect these troopers of being Mackworth's spies, sent to infiltrate the camp, a common enough practice during the Civil War.

As proof of such tactics we may again refer to John Cruso's military manual: such soldiers, 'feigning some discontent for want of pay or otherwise, [would] enter into the enemy's service, and get themselves into the cavalry. . . .' Once well established among the Heptonstall troop, they could easily relay information to Halifax by leaving messages 'at some tree, gallows, or other places easy to find.'

After much deliberation the Heptonstall command concluded that the pair were indeed deserters, who now not only supported Parliament but were also willing to turn their swords against former comrades.

Unfortunately for the two men, this change of loyalty eventually was to bring tragic consequences.

As the month unfolded disaster also appeared to await the Cheshire and Lancashire parliamentarians. Marching from Chester on 12 December, Irish troops and English royalists commanded by Lord Byron began an offensive by proceeding to Northwich, severing communications between Manchester and Nantwich, the last parliamentary stronghold in Cheshire. If this strategic town could be taken the rest of the county would capitulate, followed in all probability by an Irish invasion of Lancashire.

In these desperate circumstances Cheshire summoned help from Lancashire where Colonel Assheton was stationed. With 1500 foot he had reached Sandbach when Byron, being forewarned of his approach, sent 4000 men to intercept his advance. Against such a superior force Assheton had little choice but to begin a retreat which soon became a rout, resulting in heavy losses and the taking of many prisoners.

Byron followed his success against the Lancashire men by

Lancashire men by marching on Nantwich, which was protected only by a circuit of banks and ditches and a small defending garrison. Whether Cheshire and Lancashire remained in Parliament's hands or fell to the King would depend entirely upon the outcome of Lord Byron's siege of Nantwich.

The conflict between Sir Francis Mackworth and Major Eden at this decisive time is, sadly, unrecorded. Other than the Battle of Heptonstall and the death of Colonel Bradshaw, Brearcliffe details nothing in the final weeks of 1643. Fortunately he again took quill in hand in January 1644 to conclude the Halifax and Heptonstall story.

Perhaps in November and December his time was too much taken up with attending the wounded after the Heptonstall battle. Although most prisoners had been sent on to Rochdale, those unfit for the journey had remained behind, many to die from their injuries. If soldiers in those days did not die from their wounds, quite often they perished from shock following treatment. Many surgeons still practised old-fashioned methods of controlling bleeding by applying a red-hot poker to amputations and pouring boiling oil onto gunpowder wounds. Brearcliffe may have been one of the more progressive 'shiriugeons', using ligatures to stop bleeding and applying 'soothing creams' to wounds.

The Heptonstall parish registers contain entries for burials of a number of soldiers from the Halifax army, amongst them Jacob Williamson of Sheffield, John Stansfield of Halifax, Michael Birstow of Ovenden and Michael Butterworth, cornet.

Over a hundred civilian burials were also recorded during the occupation of Heptonstall, far in excess of numbers in times of peace.

It is difficult to imagine how, even before the war, the minister was able to officiate by the graveside in a solemn and dignified manner. His church lay at the very centre of the village and was therefore surrounded by the noise and bustle of the traders, while, only yards away, packhorses constantly clattered along the main street.

Although commercial business was now mostly halted, Towngate was used by cavalrymen and hundreds of foot soldiers who were more than capable of disturbing what should have been peaceful burial scenes.

The dead, such as Maria Crossley, a pauper, Ambrose Widdop of Crimsworth, Ann Pighilles of Wadsworth and Abraham Sunderland junior of Cragg must have been unceremoniously loaded onto carts pulled by nags and then taken up the Buttress to Heptonstall. These funeral processions were allowed entrance through the village barricades by guards who showed little emotion, for this was an almost daily occurrence.

The impoverished condition of the local populace generally, which was further weakened by repeated raiding and foraging parties from Halifax and Heptonstall alike, was all the more compounded by the onslaught of the bitter winter months. The marked rise in burial entries at Heptonstall between November 1643 and March 1644 was followed in the spring by a decline to more normal levels. But for the present the minister found himself committing to the earth a large proportion of his congregation.

Although the burial of the dead went on without interruption, the village was first and foremost a military camp. Despite a lack of information, by applying knowledge of other better-documented garrisons of a similar size and nature, a fair view may be gained of the general movements and routine activities of the Heptonstall Roundheads.

The army would have been divided equally among its three captains, each having just under 300 men to command who took the watch every third day and night. The best marksmen or 'murtherers' (usually former gamekeepers or poachers) were distributed equally throughout the ranks. Whenever the enemy was encountered it befell to them to pick off, sometimes from considerable distances, individual men or, better still, the officers. Using their own 'fouling or birding piece', their aim was often deadly accurate.

Soldiers' pay was a never-ending problem, but financial support was beginning to flow from nearby royalist landowners in Lancashire whose properties had been sequestrated and the resulting revenues diverted to their enemies, a form of robbery legalized by Act of Parliament.

The greater need was for gunpowder. With Cheshire and Lancashire in imminent danger, regular supplies from Rochdale could not be guaranteed, so to preserve stocks the captains would dispense it frugally 'and prohibit the soldier from waste of shoots'.

Patrols and sallies sometimes brought in new stocks of ammunition, as at Hollins House. Weapons were captured from ambushed enemy supply wagons or as a result of successful skirmishing, while horses, which were valuable prizes, could be seized from unwary scouts or foragers.

The rugged terrain made this type of guerilla warfare particularly effective, so that the roundheads, although insufficient in numbers to drive the cavaliers out of Halifax, could still be a sharp thorn in their sides.

Heptonstall Roundheads

At Heptonstall Major Eden's quill saw more action than his sword. Civilian matters must have taken up as much time as military concerns. Complaints against the garrison soldiers would have to be seen to be looked into, in particular those about unruly behaviour or non-payment of bills. Safe-conduct passes must be issued, as well as permits to enter and leave the village or to travel farther afield, and regular reports were sent to Rochdale, accompanied by lists of requisites.

To make a small digression: of the daily occurrences at the sister garrison upon Blackstonedge we know very little. Had Brearcliffe been stationed upon that blustery Lancashire hillside instead of at the Yorkshire outpost, our account may have been centred there.

With an army comparable in number to that at Heptonstall, and the same enemy at Halifax to contend with, similar conflicts must have taken place. Unfortunately, apart from the skirmish with Wentworth's cavalry in July 1643, the story of the Blackstonedge Garrison is largely untold.

We can only imagine the mud and the misery the soldiers endured. As Christmas approached, guarding the county border must have become increasingly tedious and uncomfortable. Yet the defence of the Lancashire pass was still an essential task, for it could not be assumed that the threat from Yorkshire had ended.

MONDAY, 25TH

> Cristo Robinson of Halifax sayeth on Christmas Day, 1643, there was a collection in Halifax Church at a communion for the poor . . . which monies Joseph Lister took away and did not dispose of it according to ye intention now otherwise.

Whether or not Mr Lister did indeed line his own pockets with the Christmas collection remains an open question. The parish poor could ill-afford the loss of charitable contributions, for their condition was such that many of them must have taken to the streets a-begging. Possibly the burden of poverty was eased by those who had helped to bring it about, the season of goodwill extending to the hearts and pockets of the Halifax Cavaliers, if only for Christmas Day.

*

There was little, if any, festive spirit in London this year, for all manner of entertainment had been banned. Even Christmas was proclaimed to be an ordinary working day, while a fast was imposed once a week so that parliamentarians should remain in the Lord's favour.

In this sombre atmosphere came news from the North of the desperate plight of Nantwich. Cheshire and Lancashire could no longer withstand the royalist assault and had sent an urgent appeal to London for assistance. The parliamentary leaders responded by calling upon their most skilful of all commanders . . .

FRIDAY, 29TH

With 1800 horse and 500 dragoons Sir Thomas Fairfax set forth from Falkingham in Lincolnshire, his destination Manchester. From there, over the next few days, he would formulate a strategy against Lord Byron and the Irish army which was besieging Nantwich.

December 1643

*

Fairfax was not alone in making mid-winter preparations, for Major Eden too was finalizing an important plan of action. No longer content with mere harassments and minor skirmishes, he now determined to attack his enemy in force.

Early the following month a fierce conflict was to occur which would be the final engagement, the last act of blood between the Halifax and Heptonstall armies.

CHAPTER SEVEN

January 1644

The Battle of Sowerby Bridge and the Hunter Hill skirmish - Sir Francis Mackworth retaliates - Major Eden's departure from Heptonstall - The Heptonstall Roundheads join Sir Thomas Fairfax at Manchester - The Scots army crosses the English border - The Battle of Nantwich - From Cheshire Colonel Lambert's forces advance towards Yorkshire - Sir Francis Mackworth's departure from Halifax

THURSDAY, 4TH

As had Colonel Bradshaw at the beginning of the campaign, Major Eden marched a force - save Captain Helliwell's company left behind to guard the camp - from Heptonstall across the valley to Sowerby village. His intention was to attack Colonel Wentworth's advanced post at Sowerby Bridge, an action designed to create maximum alarm at Halifax.

Through the usual lack of vigilance by their scouts and guards, those stationed at the bridge appear to have had little, if any, forewarning of danger and must have been dismayed at the sudden sight of an army, about 600-strong, approaching down Sowerby Hill.

Despite these overwhelming numbers and a furious onslaught, the cavaliers stoutly defended the bridge. In the hand-to-hand fighting which ensued, three of them were killed, while others were eventually beaten back and forced to surrender.

The bridge having been taken and the posts, chains and other obstacles hurriedly torn down, Captain Farrer with his cavalry galloped across to give chase to the few who had escaped, who by now were attempting to raise the alarm at King Cross.

In the meantime Major Eden's musketeers and clubmen continued to demolish the Sowerby Bridge defences. Satisfied with the day's work and without waiting for the return of Captain Farrer, the Heptonstall commander marched back to headquarters.

Although the conflict had cost the Halifax army dear, with three dead and forty-two taken prisoner (including Captain Clapham, three sergeants and two corporals), before the day's end their enemies also were to pay a severe price.

The overconfident Captain Farrer, in a manoeuvre not easily explained, ventured too far in the chase and managed to bypass the King Cross Garrison which lay directly between Halifax and Sowerby Bridge. His troop was now behind enemy lines, 'within musket shot of Halifax', and unable to rejoin Major Eden. Neither could they take the direct route back to Heptonstall, for the Roils Head and Sentry Edge outposts blocked the way. To travel with horses across country was virtually impossible: the valleys were densely wooded or marshy, while the hilltops were treacherous with spongy peat.

Nevertheless Farrer had little choice but to lead his men in a wide semicircle over the moorlands by way of Ovenden Wood, with the intention of crossing the head of Luddenden Dean. From there, with his scouts' knowledge of local tracks, it would not be difficult to reach Midgley Moor and then Heptonstall.

The Battle of Sowerby Bridge

But those who had been the pursuers suddenly found themselves the pursued. The cavalry from King Cross had at last been called to arms and now scoured the area for the enemy in their midst. Presently, the cavaliers found and followed the roundheads, intercepting them on their return to Heptonstall.

Further and further through Mixenden tired men and horses were driven off course, until finally, near Hunter Hill, at a place now known as Slaughter Gap, Captain Farrer gave the command to halt, wheel about and prepare to engage in battle. Wentworth's men likewise formed ranks, so that momentarily, with swords drawn or pistols cocked, each stared fixedly at his opponent only yards away.

Then both sides, roughly equal in numbers and totalling little more than a hundred men, were locked in combat. The royalists finally gained the upper hand, killing one and capturing ten, including Captain Farrer. The remainder made good their escape, disbanding into small groups and making their way back to Heptonstall as best they could.

The King Cross troop meanwhile rode off to deliver their prize of prisoners to Halifax, where General Mackworth undoubtedly commanded that Captain Farrer be brought before him for questioning. Little ceremony or civility attended Farrer's men, however, who were driven into dungeons, their horses, saddles, weapons, even the clothes off their backs being distributed as booty amongst their captors.

Back at Heptonstall, having witnessed the safe return of Major Eden from Sowerby Bridge, Captain Helliwell's company kept their watch throughout the day and dark hours as weary horsemen continued to arrive from Hunter Hill.

Two cavalier deserters

Despite their retreat, one group had found time to seize a civilian. As Brearcliffe tells us, 'and some going to Moor End took Mr Thompson prisoner.' Whoever the mysterious Mr Thompson was and what warranted his capture Brearcliffe does not say.

With the rout of the cavalry, comrades taken and one man killed, the Heptonstall Roundheads felt little cheer that winter's evening, despite leading what was otherwise a successful venture; while Major Eden could do little but lament over the loss of a valued officer.

But the day's dramatic events were not yet over. At Halifax, two of Captain Farrer's men had been recognized by former fellow soldiers. These were the deserters from Mackworth's army, and for their crime the whole weight of military law fell upon them.

Court martialled and found guilty of desertion, sentence was passed and carried out . . .

> 4th January, two men being soldiers were hanged on a gallows near our gibbet, which were taken by Sir Franc Mackworth's company from Heptonstall forces, which said men only run away from Halifax army unto Hept and very unhumanly put them away the same night they were taken prisoner.

This cruel act of retribution brought to a close the day which had seen the Battle of Sowerby Bridge and the Hunter Hill skirmish.

*

The following day Trooper Moore of the Heptonstall cavalry, one of those captured at Hunter Hill, died at Halifax from his wounds. Three weeks later Matthew Chester, thought to have been another of Captain Farrer's men, suffered the same fate.

As a result of the daring raid on Sowerby Bridge Sir Francis Mackworth decided that his enemies must be removed from the district once and for all. He made plans for a new assault upon Heptonstall and, to ensure success, he sent to the nearby garrison at Keighley for troops, which, some 1500-strong, duly arrived.

TUESDAY, 9TH

Reinforced, once again the Halifax Cavaliers marched out of the town. This was a confident army, well in excess of 2000 men. At the first sight of the impressive, mile-and-a-half-long column of cavalrymen and foot soldiers slowly winding its way along the moorland road, Heptonstall scouts galloped back to the village to report its advance.

Realizing his position was no longer tenable and that neither the high slopes of Heptonstall Hill nor his own small army could prevail against such a threat, Major Eden gave the command to retreat.

A flurry of activity ensued. Soldiers saddled and bridled horses, or shouldered muskets ready to form rank and file. Others loaded ammunition supplies onto carts or rounded up prisoners who were also destined to make the long march ahead.

As Mackworth's force drew ever nearer, Major Eden's men, watched by the inhabitants of a now defenceless village, began the march into Lancashire which would take them along the Long Causeway, through Stiperden to Burnley, where an overnight camp was to be made pending further orders.

As the roundhead rearguard disappeared into the distance, those villagers who had chosen to remain in Heptonstall could only apprehensively await the arrival of another army which they knew was relentlessly approaching.

Again the cavaliers massed along the bank of the river at Hebden Bridge, but as they passed over the bridge to scale the hillside they were met not by boulders and bullets, but by a perplexing silence.

The 'forlorn hope', the advance guard of General Mackworth's army, was the first to realize that the enemy had flown. Meeting no opposition, a steady stream of men marched up the Buttress and entered Heptonstall, only to find it deserted by all but a few civilians.

Although no loss of life ensued, the soldiers vented their frustration by destroying the main part of the village. Fourteen houses and barns were burned to the ground, the remaining homes pillaged and all the cattle and livestock taken.

Plumes of thick smoke, visible from many miles around, proclaimed the end of the parliamentarian presence at Heptonstall and the final, if hollow, royalist victory.

Presently, more black clouds were to appear just a few miles to the northeast as the returning Keighley forces, frustrated by a tedious and wasted journey, fired Haworth, a village much like Heptonstall, with its well-used packhorse road leading westwards into Lancashire.

Although Sir Francis Mackworth once again held undisputed control of the area, national events, which were moving very swiftly, were soon to have far-reaching and dramatic consequences, both for him and for Major Eden.

WEDNESDAY, 10TH

From Burnley Major Eden led his men to Colne. There he learned that Sir Thomas Fairfax, to strengthen his own army, had summoned to Manchester all the available foot regiments of Cheshire and Lancashire prior to marching to the relief of Nantwich.

SUNDAY, 14TH

Responding to Fairfax, the Heptonstall Roundheads returned to the town where, four months to the day, Colonel Bradshaw had originally agreed to command them. The campaign had come full circle.

Manchester was a heartening sight to men who had spent half the winter on Heptonstall Hill. The prospect of being commanded by the brilliant Fairfax may also have made up for the disappointment at having to leave their home county.

*

As Sir Thomas was making final preparations for marching into Cheshire, winter descended upon the country. Heavy snow made travel impossible and for a week his army was trapped in Manchester.

To his soldiers the delay must have been a welcome opportunity to rest and recover their strength.

During this time, as they passed the long winter nights in the snow-bound town, Major Eden's men recounted the exploits of the Heptonstall Garrison; the attack on Hollins House, the Battles of Heptonstall and Sowerby Bridge, the Hunter Hill skirmish, and other undocumented encounters with the Halifax

Cavaliers. Such tales would lose nothing in the telling and those from other regions responded with their own vivid accounts.

But the respite was to be short-lived. As soon as the thaw set in great armies began to move . . .

FRIDAY, 19TH

Parliament's allies, the Scots, crossed into England and entered the war.

SUNDAY, 21ST

Sir Thomas Fairfax, with twenty-eight troops of horse and 2500 foot, including Major Eden's soldiers, left Manchester and moved south into Cheshire.

THURSDAY, 25TH

As the parliamentarians approached Nantwich, which was on the point of surrendering, Lord Byron lifted the siege and prepared for battle.

With Fairfax before them and the town garrison making a sortie from the rear, the royalists were totally defeated. Although Byron's cavalry managed to reach the safety of Chester, his 1500-strong infantry surrendered almost to a man.

The Battle of Nantwich, which began around midday and lasted for two hours, completely destroyed the King's plans for the North.

The victorious Fairfax, not content with saving Cheshire and Lancashire, looked now to Yorkshire. Immediately after the battle he detached a force under Colonel Lambert with orders to attempt the recovery of the West Riding, beginning with Halifax.

Though not documented, it is more than likely that the Heptonstall soldiers were integrated into Lambert's army, for having fought a campaign in Yorkshire, Major Eden's knowledge of the lie of the land and of the enemy's strengths and weaknesses would have proved invaluable.

*

The following night Lambert, his men having undergone a forced march back to Lancashire, came to the garrison at Blackstonedge where he made final preparations for the long-awaited advance into Yorkshire. Gaining intelligence of these movements, General Mackworth hurriedly sent an undated letter to Colonel Wentworth at King Cross:

> I have received certain intelligence that the enemy is drawn very strong to Blackstonedge, about two thousand. I desire you would therefore, not fail to send (and see it performed) express orders for all your horse to be in readiness, and send out a very great party of two bodies that way to prevent all danger, and to come to give me notice of your endeavours when I shall give you further orders. . . . Let me know what time you have received this letter and send a company to the guard. We must look about us. . . .

Almost as soon as it was despatched, this letter was countermanded. Endeavouring to check the advance of the Scots in Northumberland, the Earl of Newcastle had been forced back to Durham, where both armies now faced each other. Unable to maintain his authority in Yorkshire, Newcastle recalled his forces there, ordering them to York, the last remaining royalist stronghold in the county.

Just as the defeat of the Fairfaxes at Adwalton Moor had brought into being our story, so would the coming of the Scots, the Fairfax victory at Nantwich and Lambert's approach from Lancashire draw it to a conclusion.

Having defended the outer garrisons for a final time, soldiers stationed at Sentry Edge, Roils Head, Sowerby Bridge and King Cross were ordered back to Halifax. As the whole army gathered in the town the mood of the men must have been very different from their arrogance back in those summer days of 1643 when Yorkshire had first fallen to Newcastle's forces.

The royalist conquest of the county was now on the verge of collapse and the King in danger of losing the war. Yet little regret was shown at the prospect of leaving a township whose inhabitants were hostile and whose lands were barren and wasted.

Soldiers' thoughts must have turned towards wives and families left behind in the Border Counties a year before. Moreover the Scottish army, having marched through Northumberland to Durham, now posed a dangerous threat in those parts. The men desired, therefore, nothing other than to leave Yorkshire and return home to defend their own lands.

SUNDAY, 28TH

As Sir Francis Mackworth rode out of Halifax towards Bradford perhaps his thoughts betrayed a certain resignation as he reflected on the previous seven months and the bitter struggle against the Heptonstall Roundheads. The future, too, appeared bleak.

In scenes similar to those at Heptonstall only three weeks

earlier, the townsfolk, having prayed many an hour for a day such as this, watched in silence as, with drums beating and banners flying, the Halifax Cavaliers marched on, leaving the town for ever.

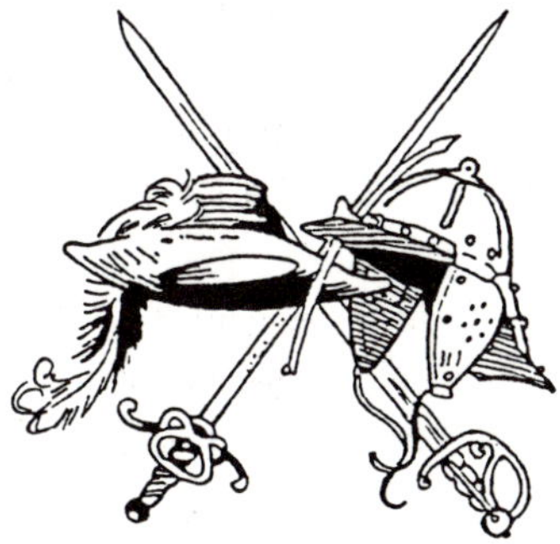

CONCLUSION

January-July 1644

Although our story rightfully ends with the last royalist soldier marching out of Halifax, if we look a little further into the first half of 1644 we find that, although embroiled in national events and integrated into two great armies, Sir Francis Mackworth's and Major Eden's soldiers were destined to meet once again, not in localized fighting or minor skirmishes, but in what was to be the largest and most important battle of England's Civil War.

JANUARY

From Halifax, Sir Francis Mackworth fell back to Bradford and Leeds en route to York. From Blackstonedge, Colonel Lambert's forces marched to Sowerby and thence to Halifax, Keighley and Bradford, liberating these important clothing towns in quick succession.

FEBRUARY

From York, Lord Bellasis, in an attempt to recapture Bradford, attacked Lambert's forces there, but was defeated and retired first to York and then to Selby.

John Brearcliffe returned home to Halifax.

Sir Thomas Fairfax reclaimed the whole of Cheshire, then,

marching into Lancashire, laid siege to the last royalist stronghold in that county, the Earl of Derby's Lathom House.

MARCH

Fairfax returned to Yorkshire.

With the Earl of Newcastle's forces in full retreat and Lancashire no longer threatened from Yorkshire, the Blackstonedge Garrison was withdrawn.

APRIL

Lord Fairfax marched out of Hull to meet his son at Ferrybridge. Their combined forces attacked and retook Selby. Lord Bellasis was wounded and taken prisoner.

Learning of this disaster, the Earl of Newcastle left Durham and retreated to York. As Major Eden had united with Fairfax at Manchester in January, so were the Earl's forces now combined with those of General Mackworth at York.

The Scots and the Fairfaxes laid siege to the city.

MAY

Prince Rupert was ordered to the relief of York. He marched north by way of Lancashire in an attempt to retake the county. Advancing on Stockport and Bolton, he bypassed Manchester which was considered too well fortified.

JUNE

Rupert stormed Liverpool, lifted the siege of Lathom House and marched to York. Consequently the siege of York was lifted.

2 JULY

Over 45,000 men engaged in the Battle of Marston Moor, which saw the defeat of Prince Rupert, the downfall of the King's cause in the North and the destruction of Newcastle's entire army.

Having allowed the Fairfaxes to slip through the net after Adwalton Moor exactly one year before, the Earl now paid a terrible price. His whitecoat infantry, including the Halifax army, resisted the enemy's onslaught to the bitter end. Refusing all offers of quarter, barely thirty men survived, among them Sir Francis Mackworth.

It is safe to assume that Major Eden fought in the battle, for the two Fairfaxes were present and Colonel Lambert also.

The Battle of Marston Moor saw not only the ruin of the Earl of Newcastle (who went into exile) and the eventual rise of Sir Thomas Fairfax to commander-in-chief of all Parliament's forces (until he was eventually eclipsed by Cromwell), but also the final engagement between the Halifax Cavaliers and the Heptonstall Roundheads.

THE END

Bibliography

E. Broxap, *The Great Civil War in Lancashire*, Manchester University Press, 1910

Halifax Antiquarian Society Transactions

T. W. Hanson, *The Story of Old Halifax*, 1920; S. R. Publishers Ltd, 1968

Winifred I. Heywood, *Yorkshire and the Civil War*, Dalesman Books, 1976

G. Ormerod (ed.), *Military Proceedings in Lancashire*, Chetham Society, 1844

Basil N. Reckett, *Charles the First and Hull*, Mr Pye Books, 1952

C. V. Wedgwood, *The King's War*, Fontana, 1966

Publisher's Note

For readers who are curious as to why this book has been dedicated to a relatively unknown officer of the English Civil War - Captain Helliwell of the Heptonstall Garrison - the following information may be of interest.

It remains the author's firm belief that the course of his life has hitherto been directed - for the specific purpose of the accomplishment of a 'mission' - by the spirit of Captain Helliwell. Such is the affinity between these two individuals that for many years David Shires has virtually been compelled to take on the very guise of his seventeenth-century counterpart. In authentic cavalryman's uniform, and astride his formidable war horse Oliver, David Shires, alias Captain Helliwell the roundhead, like a ghost from the past, may often be seen riding through Heptonstall, or pausing to rest for a while in other towns and villages throughout Yorkshire and Lancashire.

The story of this strangest of all partnerships (Mr Shires describes it as 'a true ghost story') is told, often by way of amusing or philosophical anecdotes, in a fully illustrated book entitled:

Halifax, Heptonstall and Helliwell

For further details, please contact the Puritan Press

David Shires, alias Captain Helliwell the roundhead